Israel:

Years of Challenge

DAVID BEN-GURION

Israel: Years of Challenge

Holt, Rinehart and Winston

New York   Chicago   San Francisco

Published simultaneously in Canada by Holt, Rinehart
and Winston of Canada, Limited.

Library of Congress Catalog Card Number: 63–18431

First Edition

Grateful acknowledgment is expressed to The Jewish Publication Society
of America, Philadelphia, Pennsylvania, for permission to quote excerpts
from *The Holy Scriptures According to the Masoretic Text,* Copyright,
1917, 1955 by The Jewish Publication Society of America.

Designer: Ernst Reichl
80894-0113
Printed in the United States of America

Contents

Contents

Israel:
Years of Challenge

Chapter One
Return to Zion

During the best part of a thousand years, there had been
a modest return of Jews to what was always, for them, the
Land of Israel. Piety had provided the motive in most
instances and had led, for example, to the founding at
Safad of one of the most celebrated seats of Judaic learning. Occasionally, however, the impulse to return came
from a desire to cultivate the soil itself. As early as 1563,
Don Josef Nassi led his followers from Spain to Palestine
and founded an agricultural colony in Galilee, on the
shores of Lake Tiberias. Much later, just a little over a
hundred years ago, an illustrious Jewish philanthropist
from Britain, Sir Moses Montefiore, tried to persuade the
Jews of the Holy Land to become farmers, and, for this
plan, the first Jewish orange grove was acquired near
Jaffa in 1856. After a gap of thirteen years, the Alliance
Israélite Universelle, a foundation of the Jews of France,
started the first Jewish agricultural school in Palestine,
Mikveh Yisrael, and in 1878 a Jew from the Old City of

Jerusalem, Yoel Moshe Salomon, together with the earlier Hungarian *halutzim* or pioneers, set up the first Jewish village. With profound meaning the village was named Petah Tikva, Gateway of Hope.

Later, the men of the Bilu movement from Russia and pioneers from Rumania came and built Rishon Le-Zion, Zichron Yaakov, Rosh Pina, and Gedera. Others carried forward the work, deepened and reinforced its foundations, and bound it closely to the personal labor of the settler and to a body of Jewish pioneers tilling their own soil and guarding their own farmsteads.

Some of the best of the Diaspora, calling themselves Hovevei Zion, Lovers of Zion, gave aid unsparingly to these harbingers of reconstruction. One was outstanding, a man of great vision, will, and performance, Baron Edmond de Rothschild of Paris, who deservedly won the right to be known as Father of the Yishuv or Jewish community in Palestine.

In 1896, Theodore Herzl, a Viennese playwright and journalist, who had seen in Paris the anti-Semitism of the notorious Dreyfus Case, startled progressive Jewish thinkers, young and old, with the publication of his tract *Der Judenstaat* (*The Jewish State*).

Herzl's *Der Judenstaat* proposed a self-governing Jewish community and gave to the awakening Jewish spirit an exciting goal. More than a visionary, Herzl, a year after the publication of his tract, succeeded in bringing together, at a congress in Switzerland, prominent Jewish leaders from all communities and organizations of any significance. Out of their deliberations, with Herzl as President, came the World Zionist Organization, the driving force behind a world-wide campaign to restore to the Jewish nation the right to settle in its ancient homeland.

4

There were three transcendent visionaries of the Jewish State in the nineteenth century, but only one of them, Moses Hess, linked his vision with the Land of Israel from the very beginning. Leon Pinsker, in his remarkable work, *Autoemancipation,* and even Herzl in *Der Judenstaat,* did not conceive of national redemption and solidarity only in Palestine, or there at all. In the early eighties, however, the contagion of Hibbat Zion, Love of Zion, which called for Jewish resettlement in Palestine, drew them toward the Promised Land.

Practical Zionists understood that the essential problem was how to immigrate to and settle in a country not controlled by Jews; they knew by historic instinct that they would somehow have to create a Jewish community with a stake in the Land.

Political Zionists, like Herzl and his disciples, could only see the problem of the "governor," not of the governed, and, insofar as lay in their power, they engaged in political work to win over the ruler, the Turkish Sultan. Before the First World War, the Arab countries were an integral part of the Ottoman Empire, to which the Land of Israel, like its neighbors, also belonged. Herzl foresaw the disintegration of that empire and pinned his faith on Great Britain. In 1902 he discussed with the British Government a plan to settle Jews in El Arish, in the Sinai Desert, but a water shortage as well as the disfavor of Lord Cromer, then Agent-General of the British Government in Egypt, put it out of court. Thereupon, Joseph Chamberlain, England's Secretary for Colonies, offered Uganda, an offer that split the Zionist Organization. Herzl found that, of all people, it was the Zionists of Russia, suffering the terrors of pogroms, who rebelled most vehemently against any substitute, however temporary, for the Land of Israel. He yielded to them and continued his work for the Homeland until 1904, when, at the age of forty-four, the man who foretold the Jewish State died, worn out by his selfless labors.

The urge to settle in Palestine had steadily developed and had received a certain impetus from the failure of the Russian revolution of 1905, which, if it had been successful, might have been followed by some form of Jewish emancipation throughout the Russian dominions. At any rate, a wave of immigration to Palestine began in 1904 and came to be known as the Second Aliya. (The Hebrew word *aliya* means "going up," i.e., "Going up to Zion." The First Aliya was the name given to the immigration that founded the early settlements from 1882 onward.)

It was my privilege to be one of the Second Aliya.

I was born on December 16, 1886, in Plonsk, a small town of Polish origin but at that time a part of the Russian Empire. My father, who practiced law, was a fervent supporter of the Hovevei Zion movement, and our house was a meeting place for the more progressive Jews of the town, who would gather there to discuss the prospects of emigration and settlement in Palestine. Naturally, I imbibed, from an early age, my father's zealous longing for the emancipation of the Jews and their return to Zion.

Much of my early youth was spent trying to persuade others to think as I did, and I took an active part in such relevant organizations as were at hand, notably Poalei Zion, or Workers of Zion, which can fairly be described as the forerunner of the great labor organization, the Histadrut.

In 1906, at the age of nineteen, I decided that organizing Zionist groups and delivering ardent speeches in towns and villages was not enough. The time had come to contribute as best I could, in the Land of Israel itself, to

6

laying the foundations for the return of my people to their Homeland.

That summer, some friends and I boarded a Russian tramp steamer bound for the eastern Mediterranean. We had managed to get Turkish visas permitting us to remain in Palestine for a period of three months, but we had no intention of leaving, if we could possibly help it. Two weeks after we left Russia, Jaffa hove in sight. It was an exalting occasion and as we landed on the sacred shores, and I felt that my heart would burst. Of that event I have written:

> We had left behind our books and our theorizing, the hairsplitting and the argument, and come to the Land to redeem it by our labor. We were all still fresh; the dew of dreams was still moist in our hearts; the blows of reality had still to sober our exalted spirit.

The blows were not long in falling; those first years were laborious and often frustrating. Among the early disappointments was the spectacle of Jews of the First Aliya, now living as *effendis*, drawing their income from groves and fields worked by hired workmen, or from occupations of the kind imposed on our people by their exile. It was clear to me that we could never achieve national rehabilitation that way. Between the land and the people, there had to be the bond of labor.

Today, many do not know that less than half a century ago there was a stern and seemingly hopeless struggle for the right of Jews to work in the Homeland. In 1912, Asher Ginzberg, distinguished philosophical essayist and exponent of "Spiritual Zionism," using the pen name Ahad Ha'am, wrote:

7

. . . We must reconcile ourselves to the idea that our rural population in the Land of Israel, even if in the course of time it expands to the very limit of possibility, will always be an upper-class population, a highly-developed and cultural minority, and strong only in intellect and wealth. There will be no population of countryfolk, mighty of muscle. By this the character and purpose of Zionism are altered out of recognition. . . .

Two generations of pioneers, shrinking from no hardship, capitulating to no degrading reality, disproved the pessimistic forecast of the greatest thinker of Hovevei Zion. Jewish labor has gained a place in every branch of work, just as Hebrew has conquered school and street and become the vernacular again. There has grown up, not an "upper-class" population, but a community with its strength in its toil, its spirit and its sinews. Pioneer aliya gave birth to a Jewish community radically unlike all others, independent in economy, culture, and speech, able to defend itself. It was this community that blazed a trail for the greatest event in our history since the conquests of Joshua, son of Nun, and of David, son of Jesse: the birth of the State of Israel.

For myself, I labored in grove and vineyard and wine press, later joining the farming settlement of Sejera in Galilee. There I followed the plow, and as the black clods of earth turned and crumbled, and the oxen trod with the slow and heedless dignity of their kind, I saw visions and dreamed dreams. We were still hardly more than a handful; but young, eager pioneers of the Second Aliya continued to land at Jaffa and to spread throughout the land.

Certainly, each of our small communities needed a

8

sense of organization; we had to become thoroughly self-reliant groups, capable, even, of our own defense against marauders. Arab bandits were most active at night, and at Sejera we began training ourselves as guards. A night-watch system was gradually adopted by all our settlements, and out of the Hashomer (Watchman) organization sprang, at a later date when Arab hostility developed into widespread armed raiding, the secretly trained and partially armed defense organization known as the Hagana, which was the source of our strength when the State was founded and five Arab armies descended upon us. Out of the Hagana grew the armed forces of the State of Israel.

In the days at Sejera, we were only at the beginning. We had steadily organized ourselves, but we were few in number and our status was uncertain. Subjects of the Ottoman Sultan in Constantinople, we knew that any concessions to our national aims, such as the recognition of Hebrew as our national tongue, could come only from the Turkish authorities. A knowledge of Turkish law and habits of negotiation, as well as the Turkish language, seemed necessary to those of us who saw the need for political activities to strengthen our position in the country. Therefore my good friend and colleague, the late Izhak Ben-Zvi, and I decided to go to Constantinople to study Ottoman law and learn Turkish.

With our object only partially achieved, World War I began, and Ben-Zvi and I returned to Jerusalem to find many of our people fleeing the city. We were thrown into jail as potential conspirators against the Turkish Empire and then, without a trial, expelled. Our next destination was Alexandria, where the British regarded us as enemy subjects but finally permitted us to move on to the United States, for which we had been given visas.

We arrived in New York in the spring of 1915 and stumped the country, spreading the pioneering ideal and urging young Jews to undergo agricultural training to fit themselves to be workers and settlers in the Palestine that would emerge from the war. We persuaded our own political group, Poalei Zion, and such influential Zionists as Louis D. Brandeis, later a Justice of the United States Supreme Court, to advocate the setting up of a Jewish military unit to fight against Turkey and to participate in the liberation of Palestine. The United States was not at war with Turkey, of course, and it was Britain which, after some negotiation, agreed to the formation of a Jewish legion and incorporated it in the Middle East armies under General Edmund Allenby (later Lord Allenby). However, we were permitted to recruit men for the Legion in the United States.

For Zionists, 1917 was a climacteric year. Allenby's army, with its Jewish battalions—the first of their kind since the revolt of the Jews against the Romans in the year 135—was marching on Palestine. Almost simultaneously with Allenby's victorious progress toward Jerusalem, in November, 1917, came news of that heartening British document, the Balfour Declaration, which stated that

His Majesty's Government view with favour the establishment in Palestine of a national home for the Jewish people, and will use their best endeavours to facilitate the achievement of this object, it being clearly understood that nothing shall be done which may prejudice the civil and religious rights of existing non-Jewish communities in Palestine or the rights and political status enjoyed by Jews in any other country.

The attainment of this declaration must be credited, in major part, to the political efforts of Dr. Chaim Weizmann, later the first President of Israel, who in 1917 already held a leading place in Zionist affairs and, as a chemist, had rendered signal service to the British war effort.

In 1915, two years before the Declaration, Sir Henry McMahon, the British High Commissioner in Egypt, had made certain commitments to Sherif Hussein of Mecca, purportedly promising British liberation of the Arab lands from the Turkish Empire and the crowning of the Sherif as king over them. The area of Palestine was specifically excluded from the pledge, but Weizmann, an experienced statesman, could not ignore the political aspirations of the Arabs, and he sought, with success, both the Balfour Declaration and an agreement with Feisal, son of the Sherif of Mecca.

On January 3, 1919, Weizmann and Feisal signed a compact of friendship between Jewish Palestine and the Arab state which would be its neighbor. In part the compact stated:

> Immediately following the completion of the deliberations of the [Versailles] Peace Conference, the definite boundaries between the Arab State and Palestine shall be determined. . . . In the establishment of the Constitution and Administration of Palestine, all such measures shall be adopted as will afford the fullest guarantees for carrying into effect the British Government's declaration of November 2, 1917 [the Balfour Declaration]. All necessary measures shall be taken to encourage and stimulate the immigration of Jews into Palestine on a large scale and as quickly as possible, and to settle Jewish immigrants upon the land. . . .

11

Two months later Feisal wrote to Justice Felix Frankfurter, then an American member of the Zionist delegation at the Peace Conference:

> We Arabs, especially the educated among us, look with the deepest sympathy on the Zionist movement. Our deputation here in Paris is fully acquainted with the proposals submitted by the Zionist Organization to the Peace Conference, and we regard them as moderate and proper. We will do our best, in so far as we are concerned, to help them through; we all wish the Jews a most hearty welcome home. . . .
>
> I look forward, and my people with me look forward, to a future in which we will help you and you will help us, so that countries in which we are mutually interested may once again take their place in the community of civilized peoples of the world.

But the Feisal-Weizmann agreement had no practical value. In Palestine and in the neighboring countries, even in Iraq, where Feisal had been crowned king, the Arabs either ignored or denied the intent of the agreement.

In April, 1920, at the Conference of the Allied Powers in San Remo, Italy, the fate of the dismembered Turkish Empire was considered, and the Allied Supreme Council assigned the Mandate for Palestine to Great Britain. However, it had to be ratified officially by the League of Nations, and it was not until July, 1922, that the Council of the League gave the Mandate its official endorsement. Weizmann was obliged to rely exclusively on the Balfour Declaration and on the Mandate, and in consequence he focused his political attention on Britain. However, he never forgot the Arab problem or wearied of stressing the

12

advantage that Jewish settlement in Palestine could bring the Arabs.

From the start, Zionist ideology was ruled by the thesis that the return of the Jews to their Land was bound up with a lofty mission to make the Middle East bloom again and to establish friendly co-operation between two Semitic peoples which, in the Middle Ages, had together been the torchbearers of progress and science.

At the Zionist Congress in 1933, the labor bloc delegates were led by Mapai, the Labor party of the Land of Israel. For the first time, it was the largest group, and I, as its representative, was elected to the Executive of the Zionist Organization and the Jewish Agency,* becoming Chairman of the Executive two years later. It seemed to me that our principal task was to expand immigration as speedily as possible, but I could not, any more than Weizmann, afford to shelve the Arab question. In an attempt to find some common formula for Zionism and its aspirations and for Arab nationalism, I entered into conversations with prominent Palestinian Arabs and with representatives of Syria, Lebanon, Egypt, and Saudi Arabia.

In preparation for my meetings with the Arabs, I spoke to the High Commissioner, General Sir Arthur Wauchope, a very true friend of the Zionist cause, and asked him if the British Government would back a Jewish-Arab accord should I succeed in negotiating one. With characteristic honesty, he replied that he was not authorized to speak in his Government's name, for he had no instructions, but so far as he understood its mind, he was cer-

* In the Palestine Mandate, the Zionist Organization was recognized as "an appropriate Jewish Agency for the purpose of advising and cooperating with the Administration in matters affecting the Jewish National Home and the interests of the Jewish population in Palestine." In 1929 an enlarged Jewish Agency was formed.

13

tain it would. Dr. Judah Magnes, the first Chancellor of the Hebrew University of Jerusalem, helped a great deal in arranging my talks with the Arabs, though he and I were divided in our views on Zionist questions. The talks went on for more than two years in Palestine, in the neighboring countries, and in Geneva, headquarters of the Palestine-Syria Committee. They were conducted in a friendly atmosphere but led to no results whatsoever.

While the talks were being held, an external factor intensified local antagonisms. In 1933, the National Socialist regime under Adolf Hitler was set up in Germany, and soon afterwards a systematic oppression of Jews, unheard of in the long and grievous history of Jewish persecution, began. A tide of Jewish refugees was set flowing from Germany and Austria to Palestine. In 1935, more than 60,000 Jewish immigrants entered the country. There was a clamor of protest from the Arabs, who, in 1936, began organized, murderous attacks on Jewish communities. Their assaults grew in ferocity.

In February, 1937, at a meeting in Tel Aviv of the Council of the Histadrut, the General Federation of Jewish Labor in Palestine (now the Israel General Federation of Labor), I explained why our efforts to reach a Jewish-Arab accord had been unavailing. The principal reason, it seemed to me, was our own weakness. We were not yet strong enough to be sought after as an ally. To be, in others' eyes, worthy partners in an alliance, we had to be a power.

I knew that demonstrating the justice of our national cause would not win over the Arabs. We had to get used to seeing things as the Arabs saw them. Certainly there was no reason to believe that the Arabs would align themselves with us for some dim principle of justice. They could only become "Jewish-orientated" if we could prove that there were economic and political benefits for them. We had to make them understand that the presence of the Jews in Palestine was not a feeble and fleeting factor but a decisive one, an historical reality which could not be annulled or upset or disregarded.

In November, 1936, England had sent a Royal Commission, headed by Lord Peel, to investigate Jewish-Arab relations in Palestine. The report of the Commission, issued the following year, advocated the partitioning of Palestine into a Jewish state and an Arab state with certain places, among them Jerusalem, to remain under British control. The Congress decided to empower the Executive to conduct negotiations in order to clarify the precise content of the British Government's proposal regarding the formation of a Jewish State in the Land of Israel. The British Government initially approved that proposal but later abandoned it.

At a Palestine conference, attended by Jewish and Arab representatives, called by the British Government early in 1939, the Arabs made plain their intransigent attitude toward both the Mandate and the Partition Plan, as it came to be known. The fact that, in addition to the representatives of Palestine, Arab officials from Egypt, Saudi Arabia, Iraq, and Trans-Jordan had also been invited indicated which way the wind was blowing. Neville Chamberlain, Britain's Prime Minister, was relentlessly pursuing his policy of appeasing Hitler and the Nazis, and there was every evidence that the same policy was being extended to the Arabs.

The British official statement known as the White Paper of 1939 was the result. This infamous document declared, at the very moment when millions of European Jews were facing merciless destruction, that within the next five years only 75,000 Jews would be allowed into

15

Palestine, and that thereafter none would be admitted without Arab consent. It proclaimed the building of the Jewish Homeland completed, and made the further purchase of land by Jews impossible in almost all parts of the country.

Strong voices all over the world rose in denunciation of the White Paper, the strongest being the voice of Winston Churchill in the British Parliament itself. He termed the White Paper "another Munich" and "a plain breach of a solemn obligation." World Jewry was united in its opposition.

In 1939 the Second World War broke out. The responsible heads of the Yishuv, the Jewish community in Palestine, and of the Zionist Movement realized that the Jewish people could not be neutral. The Arab rulers sided with the Nazis, contentedly recognizing in Hitler the most bloodthirsty and brutal enemy of the Jews in the pages of history. The Jews were bound in duty to take their stand with those who fought him. That obligation did not invalidate a second duty, which was to continue our struggle against the White Paper. Our task was to help the British against Hitler as though there were no White Paper and to resist the White Paper as though there were no war.

Immigration, legal or "illegal," with or without the consent of the Mandatory authorities, was not suspended but conducted with increased vigor. At the same time, 25,000 of our young men and women enlisted voluntarily in the Jewish units of the British army. The first Jewish artillery unit was formed, and eventually a whole Jewish brigade campaigned against German and Italian columns in Europe and helped refugees from Nazi ruin to make their way to safety in Palestine.

In Palestine, the Jewish community had been continu-

16

ously served by our volunteer underground defense corps, the Hagana, organized in the early 1920's and made up of most of our able-bodied young men and women. At the outbreak of war, the Hagana assumed the task of organizing immigration into Palestine and intensified all its tasks in connection with the protection and extension of Jewish settlement. In the summer of 1942, when the German General Erwin Rommel neared the gates of Egypt, a striking force called the Palmach was formed with the approval of the British authorities. Its task would be to fight behind the enemy lines if Palestine were invaded. The young soldiers of Palmach were recruited for a fixed term of two years and devoted half their time to military exercises and half to agricultural training. This, then, was the "regular" army of the Jews of Palestine during the last seven years of the Mandate —recognized and in the open until the Rommel danger had passed and then forced underground again.

The question that absorbed us was Palestine's future after the war. I was certain that we had to exert ourselves to set up a Jewish State. It was already evident that Britain would not keep the Mandate. Churchill, who had protested vehemently against the White Paper, had succeeded Chamberlain as Prime Minister—but still no change in the White Paper policy was discernible. There was sufficient ground for confidence that Hitler would be overthrown, but it was also evident that Britain, though victorious, would emerge from the conflict weakened. Even if good will were not lacking, Britain would not be strong enough to take up the Mandate again in its original interpretation or to pursue the Partition Plan.

I no longer doubted that the center of gravity of our political work in the international arena had shifted from Britain to the United States, which had firmly grasped world leadership and in which the largest and most influential Jewish concentration in the Diaspora was to be found. Europe was wholly in the Nazi grip. Hitler would in time be beaten and destroyed, but the strength of Europe would be undermined and its existence dependent for many years on America's economic aid. Even the resolution of political problems would turn on an active American part in the fighting and in the peace settlement.

In 1940, when Britain still battled on alone, I went to the United States in my capacity as Chairman of the Zionist Executive and sought to impress on the Zionist Organization of America the urgency of political campaigning, of formulating a political program and mobilizing American Jewry toward its ends. My plan was based on three things: opposition to the policy of the White Paper, the formation of a Jewish army, and the conversion of Palestine into a Jewish Commonwealth after the war.

In May, 1942, a congress of American Zionists unanimously endorsed the proposals I had advocated, under the title of the Biltmore Program, named after the hotel where the congress was held. The program contained this declaration:

The new world order that will follow victory cannot be established on foundations of peace, justice and equality unless the problem of Jewish homelessness is finally solved. The conference demands that the gates of Palestine be opened; that the Jewish Agency be vested with control of immigration into Palestine and with the necessary authority for upbuilding the country, including the development of uncultivated and unsettled areas; and that Palestine be established as a

18

Jewish commonwealth integrated into the structure of the new democratic world.

Within a year or two, some of the most important Jewish organizations in America, including the B'nai B'rith Organization, the American Jewish Committee, the Jewish Labor Committee, and the American Jewish Congress, had also approved the program.

The war ended, and Britain had neither the capacity nor the wish to exercise the Mandate as it should be exercised, and certainly not to establish a Jewish State in even a fragment of Palestine. In the first postwar elections, the British Labor party was returned to power. The Laborites had adopted far-reaching resolutions during the war in favor of a Jewish State, even presenting an extreme claim which the Jewish Agency itself had never put forward: the wholesale transplantation of the Arabs of the Jewish State to Arab countries.

A Zionist conference was held in London in August, 1945, and I felt constrained, after cataloguing gratefully the help British Labor had given Zionism over the years, to sound a gloomy warning:

Do not rely too much on this sweeping change in Britain, on this victory of the Labor party. You must not imagine that the question of the White Paper is answered by that alone.

First of all, even if we suppose that the Labor party in office will take the same stand as it did out of office, we must remember the wide gap between the two attitudes to Zionism: for us it is a central, pressing, and primary concern; for the British it is one of many and diverse issues. We cannot wait; the British have all the time in the world.

19

Second, the assumption that a party in office behaves exactly as it does out of office is highly debatable. Among us there are also those who do not practice precisely what they preach. We cannot be sure that, when it takes over, the party will demand of itself what it demanded of others a little while back and stand by it.

And third, in Britain, as is perhaps the case elsewhere, power is not in the exclusive hands of the elected government; there is a permanent Civil Service, and the colonial personnel, for the most part, constitutes a strong anti-Zionist factor. It has conducted itself as such ever since the Balfour Declaration and is not going to be dislodged now. Let us not minimize its authority and influence even under a Labor Government. The question is: the White Paper or a Jewish State? That is the acid test, and only so shall we judge the new British policy.

My misgivings were soon confirmed, and to a degree far more alarming than I had believed possible. Bitterly, even from this distance of time, we must deplore the policy of Ernest Bevin as Foreign Secretary, with Clement Attlee as Prime Minister behind him. All hope vanished that Britain might abide by its commitments. It was clear to any realist that unless we succeeded in establishing a Jewish State by our own initiative, we would remain an oppressed minority in an Arab country. It was, of course, essential to make our case known throughout the world, especially in the United States. However, I was convinced that the determining factor would be Jewish strength; we would have to be prepared, armed, and marshaled to establish and defend the State. One other thing was clear to me: we must expect conflict not only with the Arabs of Palestine but with the neighboring Arab countries as well. The Jews of Palestine and the Zionist Movement would have to be trained to pass this perilous test; we had to achieve military readiness for coming events.

Until the first Zionist Congress after the war, in 1946, I had not accepted any special portfolio on the Executive but functioned only as its Chairman. That postwar congress created a portfolio of Defense and entrusted it to me. One of my first tasks was a thorough investigation into the fighting capacity of the Hagana, its equipment, its training, and its capacity to meet the imminent challenge. I examined the arms at its disposal in April, 1947. This is what I found:

10,073 rifles (8,720 in the settlements for local defense; 336 in reserve; 656 with the Palmach brigade; 361 with the field force)

1,900 submachine guns (785 in the settlements; 424 with the field force; 130 with Palmach; 561 in reserve)

186 machine guns (31 in the settlements; 35 with the field force; 5 with Palmach; 115 in reserve)

444 light machine guns (338 in the settlements; 37 with the field force; 33 with Palmach; 46 in reserve)

The so-called heavy equipment consisted of 672 two-inch mortars and 96 three-inch mortars. There was not a single cannon, and only one heavy machine gun. There was no anti-tank weapon or anti-aircraft gun, no armored car, and nothing at all for naval or air combat. There was no communications equipment.

To assemble this pitifully small arsenal, a tremendous effort had been necessary. Transport from overseas and delivery in Palestine called for the subtlest planning and the most careful organization. *Ta'as*, the homemade ordnance factory of the Hagana, dating back to before the First World War, could produce only primitive arms, for its work had to be done clandestinely and at moral risk. The output was barely enough for the Hagana in its struggle with marauders and terrorists; it could in no way measure up to the needs of a struggle with an army of regulars or even irregulars.

As soon as the Second World War was over, I applied myself to the procurement of heavy arms, which would enable us to face a regular army, and to the construction of proper ordnance factories so that we could match the Arab armies, if we had to. In June, 1945, with Eliezer Kaplan, the Treasurer of the Jewish Agency (later, Israel's first Minister of Finance), I gathered together a group of dependable men in the United States, which was about to reduce its arms industry. I explained to our friends that the near future might see us locked in combat with the Arab armies and that we had to set up a munitions industry and acquire modern machinery for making weapons. They responded readily, and Engineer Haim Slavin was asked to come from Palestine to the United States to look after the purchasing. For less than a million dollars we bought machinery worth scores of millions, and it was all safely conveyed to Palestine. The Mandatory Government, for all the zeal with which it then instituted searches for arms in Jewish settlements, never once detected its nature or purpose.

The two countries which agreed to sell us arms were Czechoslovakia and France. Part of the matériel, including rifles, machine guns, and a number of field pieces, arrived secretly by air a short time before the State was established. However, most of the equipment could be brought in only after the founding of the State, and

22

the commissioning of the greater part of the machinery also had to wait until then. In the fighting before and immediately after the establishment of the State, we had, therefore, to defend ourselves with arms inferior to the enemy's in quality as well as in quantity. Only in mid-June of 1948 and later did arms of all types begin to reach the Israel Defense Forces.

The fact that the Hagana, from its inception, had always been a volunteer organization was a circumstance of incalculable importance. A volunteer has an immense advantage over a conscript. In every army, of course, there is comradeship in arms, but comradeship imposed by law and authority is nothing like the kind that men distill of their own free choice out of a common mission in life. That is why the members of the Hagana demonstrated such limitless devotion to the security of the Yishuv. The strength of an army is measured not alone by the caliber of its equipment and training, though these are not to be dismissed lightly, but also by a spiritual readiness to resist to the last and never to give in. This, stronger than death itself, had been the Hagana's great virtue, carrying forward the spirit of Hashomer, which protected the first Jewish settlements.

In July, 1947, as Minister of Defense within the Zionist Executive, I issued instructions to the Hagana formations. Among others, I made the following statements:

> The political threat is still there; in fact, it is worse than ever. The anti-Zionist and anti-Jewish designs of the White Paper Government are becoming increasingly patent. Also, the Arab threat is back, and on a much larger scale. This time there await us not only "disturbances" stirred up by the Arab leadership in

23

Palestine, but also aggression led by the rulers of the Arab states—and we had better lose no time in getting ourselves ready to face this threat.

These two threats—the British and the Arab—feed on each other. The anti-Zionist policy of the Mandatory Government encourages the Arab hostility, eggs it on, activates it, and supports it. And Arab belligerency grows with the help and encouragement it receives—moral, political, and material help (in the form of military training and equipment)—from the British Government.

Yet we must distinguish between these two threats. The quarrel of Zionism with the White Paper is fundamentally political and not military, and the military action that must sometimes be resorted to in this political struggle is intended only to strengthen our political position. In this struggle the Hagana is only one factor; and only a total, concerted effort of Palestinian and world Jewry—in agricultural settlement and "illegal" immigration, the armed struggle, and the political struggle in the international arena—will bring us victory.

Arab aggression is quite another matter. Here the Hagana will be the main factor and the decisive one. Armed Arab aggression can be met only with force, and no outcome is possible but one brought about by Jewish arms. Unless, therefore, the Hagana is ready and fit to bring about such an outcome, it will have failed to fulfill its purpose and Jewish Palestine and the Zionist effort will face disaster.

For the time being armed gangs are operating against us only for loot, and the murders and rapes they commit have as yet no political purpose. However, it is only a short step from brigandage to butchery, and the gangs are at any moment apt to be turned into a terrorist tool manipulated by the Mufti's "political" hands.

A greater menace looms, however. We must expect openly or covertly hostile acts by the armed forces of the Arab States. Egypt, Iraq, Lebanon, Syria, and Trans-Jordan have under arms a total of more than 120,000 men of various classes and qualities of training and equipment. The best of them all, in both training and equipment, is the Trans-Jordanian army, financed entirely by Britain and now under the command of British officers. This army has the latest equipment and is very highly trained.

To train the Hagana to meet this threat and successfully to defend not only Jewish settlements and the Palestine Jewish community but also the entire land and our national future in the land—this is the critical task of the hour.

In May, 1947, the Palestine problem had been discussed in a special session of the General Assembly of the United Nations. For the first time the Jewish people, even before it had a state, had been allowed to appear in an international forum. While the League of Nations existed, the Jewish Agency could only submit its complaints in writing through the High Commissioner for Palestine; it was not even granted the right to attend sessions of the Mandates Commission, which year after year discussed the report of the Mandatory Government. Now representatives of the Jewish Agency were privileged not merely to present a statement to the United Nations but also to take part in the discussions of the Political Committee.

In the Assembly debate the basic question arose: Was the Palestine problem linked with the problem of the

Jewish people, or should the two issues be completely separated, as the Arab member states demanded? Afghanistan, Turkey and India supported the Arab view, but all the other member states dissented. Out of these deliberations came an investigation committee of eleven, excluding nominees of the Great Powers and of the Arab states, and this body, the United Nations Special Committee on Palestine (UNSCOP), was instructed to examine the Palestine problem in all its aspects and to inquire into all related questions, both in Israel and in any other place it found fitting to visit.

The great surprise of the Assembly was the appearance of Andrei Gromyko on behalf of the Soviet Union. Apart from what had been said in the White House by President Harry Truman, no positive statement had yet been made by any major country. However, Mr. Gromyko spoke of Jewish suffering, of our indescribable decimation in the war, of the dependent status and hopeless prospects of hundreds of thousands of Jews in Europe who sought asylum in vain. The political significance of his speech lay in the conclusion he drew from his analysis of the situation: the right of the Jewish people to a country of its own.

It would be unjust [he declared] if we failed to take into account this aspiration of the Jews to a state of their own and denied them the right to realize it. The withholding of that right cannot be justified, particularly when we consider all that happened to them in the Second World War. The investigation of this aspect of the problem and the formulation of suitable proposals ought, therefore, to constitute an important task of the Committee.

On September 1, 1947, the conclusions of the Committee were published. Some of its recommendations were unanimous, and there were also majority and minority recommendations. The most important unanimous recommendations were these: the earliest possible termination of the Mandate and the earliest practicable grant of independence to Palestine, with a prior period of transition which should be as brief as possible, the administration during the interregnum to be responsible to the United Nations. The Committee as a whole observed that, as it was completely impossible to devise an arrangement acceptable in its entirety to Jews as well as Arabs, imposition upon both was, so to speak, a basic condition of any proposal it could recommend; accordingly, a transitional link with the United Nations was essential. Not one member proposed that another Mandatory should take Britain's place or suggested an international mandate, which was what the left wing of Palestine labor asked for.

A majority of the Committee recommended partition and the establishment of independent Jewish and Arab states, to be joined in an economic union.

After a long and stormy discussion, more than two-thirds of the Assembly decided to accept the majority recommendations, with certain unimportant amendments. On November 29, 1947, thirty-three member states, including the United States and the Soviet Union, voted in favor of the recommendations; thirteen voted against them: six Arab states (Egypt, Syria, Lebanon, Iraq, Saudi Arabia, and Yemen), four non-Arab Moslem states (Afghanistan, Pakistan, Iran, and Turkey), and India, Greece, and Cuba; while ten abstained, Britain among them. The Arabs announced, both before the resolution

27

was adopted and after, that they would fight it tooth and nail.

In Palestine and in the Diaspora the resolution was greeted with wild enthusiasm, by Zionists and non-Zionists alike, by the pious and the non-observant, by the right and by the left. While rejoicing seized the whole House of Israel, there were deep anxieties in my own heart.

Chapter Two

Independence Reborn

Supreme international sanction had been given to the revival of a free and independent Jewish State in its ancient Homeland, but I was deeply concerned over two factors of extreme gravity. First, the pitifully small slice of territory allotted to us excluded Jerusalem and confined us to narrow strips of coastal territory, a part of Galilee, and a broad area of the barren Negev, much of it intricately woven among lands included in the proposed Arab state, and dependent on narrow corridors for the maintenance of communications. Second, the plan was rejected by the Arabs, who made ominous threats to stop at nothing to prevent the implementation of any part of it.

Small and fragmentary as the area allotted to us was, nevertheless we were willing to make the best of it. What caused me deep anxiety were my doubts about the capacity and willingness of the United Nations to implement its own resolution, the terms of which were not merely a recommendation but regarded as juridically blinding on the peoples directly concerned and on all member states of the United Nations; and my further doubts about the preparedness of the 650,000 Jews in Palestine to defend themselves against all armies of the neighboring Arab states if the United Nations should fail to impose its will. Although the boundaries of the Jewish State as drawn in the Partition Resolution nowhere impinged on the lands of any existing Arab state, it became clear, from the moment Great Britain expressed its intention of surrendering the Mandate and submitting the problem of Palestine to the United Nations Organization, that the setting up of a Jewish State in the country would be met by the active hostility not of the Palestine Arabs alone but also of the organized and well-armed adjoining Arab states.

The finest military unit in the Middle East at that time was the Trans-Jordan Arab Legion, which in effect was under British command and was stationed in Palestine. Britain was also in evidence in Egypt and in Iraq. British officers either trained or commanded the armies of these states, and British armament was being used in most Arab countries, Syria and Lebanon excepted. Only unthinking fervor could breed the notion that the Assembly's resolution had solved the problem, and that the Jewish State would arise untroubled in its own good time and in obedience to international directives.

The defense of the Yishuv was my particular responsibility and one that filled me with foreboding. The Hagana, made up of dedicated men as it undoubtedly was, and trained in such arms as we had been able to procure, was no match for the armed forces of our potential enemies. If we should be compelled to mobilize every available man, there would not be enough weapons to go round. We had no heavy armament; no navy; above all, no

30

air force. As I have explained, we had succeeded in placing with France and Czechoslovakia orders for essential armament, equipment and machinery for our own arsenals, and some deliveries had been made. The question now was whether we would succeed in getting further urgent deliveries in time to meet a combined Arab onslaught. It seemed unlikely, of course, that the neighboring Arab states would march to the attack so long as the British remained at least in nominal control of the country.

The British delegate at the plenary session of the U.N. General Assembly, Sir Alexander Cadogan, had declared:

> I can assure the General Assembly that, if the present draft resolution is adopted, my Government will loyally accept it in so far as its terms do not conflict with the conditions laid down in the Colonial Secretary's speech of 26th September 1947 and in subsequent statements made by my delegation.

On January 14 Sir Alexander told the U.N. Implementation Committee that his Government

> will endeavour to give the Commission the benefit of their experience and knowledge of the situation in Palestine, subject always to their decision that they are unable to take part in the implementation of the United Nations' plan.

What these statements meant in practice we were soon to learn.

The Arabs were not tardy. On November 30, 1947, they opened their terrorist campaign in Palestine. An

Arab gang ambushed Jewish travelers and murdered seven. On December 1, the Arab Executive Committee decided on a three-day strike in protest against the resolution and on a day of demonstrations when the Assembly adjourned. On December 2, the strike began; an Arab mob set fire to the Jewish commercial center in Jerusalem. The British police stood by; all they did was to hinder the Hagana from coming to the rescue of Jews under attack. The Arabs of Ramleh, a town on the Tel Aviv-Jerusalem road, fell upon Jewish passers-by, and the police stopped traffic between Jerusalem and Tel Aviv. The Mandatory Government was proving itself ineffectual. I gave instructions that the ban on movement between Jerusalem and Tel Aviv was to be disregarded, for honoring it simply meant official support for the hostile acts of the Arab Higher Executive Committee.

In early December, there began a withdrawal of Arabs from the area assigned to the Jewish State. They decamped from Haifa and other towns and from the Sharon Valley, which lies along the coast south of Haifa. Their leaders got away to Nablus, which lies in a line straight north of Jerusalem in an area that was to be part of the Arab state. The flight was still mainly of women and children, but many men also took to their heels. This went on until the State of Israel was established. Many villages were entirely emptied. Most of the northern Beduin Arabs shifted their tents to the Arab area and a few to the Jewish Negev in the south. Only from Galilee, the region stretching across the northernmost part of our country, was there no significant Arab exodus.

Meanwhile the Arabs of Jaffa, Jerusalem, Haifa, Lod, and Ramleh grew more bellicose. A fortnight after the U.N. resolution, the Arab League met in Cairo and decided to dispatch military columns to Palestine for guerilla actions. This penetration by foreign combatants met with no resistance from the Mandatory Government, which, nonetheless, went on protesting that until the Mandate ended it alone was responsible for law and order. It even refused to co-operate with the United Nations Commission appointed to ease the passage from Mandate to independence.

At first, Arab violence was confined to Jerusalem, Jaffa, and the Tel Aviv-Jerusalem highway. The British police, in the main, took up positions with the Arabs. The Hagana did its best to localize clashes and avoid arguments with British troops, but we knew that the real test would come when the British left. Only if we were then properly armed could we handle the Arab armies.

For months, we kept up defensive tactics, but, as Arab assaults grew more vicious and the plan to cut off Jerusalem from the rest of the Yishuv and block the Tel Aviv-Jerusalem route gained headway, we were compelled to go over to the offensive. The tempo of the Yishuv's mobilization was accelerated. The Arabs were getting reinforcements from neighboring countries, and attacks both by Palestinian gangs and by irregulars from outside became more frequent. The Arabs realized that the surrender, seizure, or destruction of Jewish Jerusalem would shatter our fortitude and resistance. All along the route, from Abu Kabir and Salameh near Tel Aviv to Castel and Lifta on the outskirts of Jerusalem, death lurked in ambush for every Jewish traveler.

We had more than three hundred villages scattered up and down the country. Each had to be protected, including some completely isolated spots such as the Kfar Etzion bloc of settlements in the Hebron hills south of Jerusalem, Yehiam in Galilee, Hartuv adjoining the Jerusalem corridor, and Ben Shemen on the eastern fringe of the area close to the Arab concentration in the central part of the country. It was impossible to keep them safe without lines of communication between villages and towns, and all roads were in Arab hands.

Only in Haifa did we have the upper hand all along, because that city was surrounded by Jewish settlements. At the end of January, 1948, I learned that the Arabs there were in despair: the Jewish suburb of Hadar Hacarmel, on the slopes of Mount Carmel, overlooked the Christian and Moslem quarters, and the Jews were better armed. Arab merchants were urging the Arab Executive Committee to preserve the local peace. Arabs with means were escaping to Lebanon, and others hurried off to Nazareth and south to Jenin, close to the Jordan border; already more than 25,000 had left Haifa. An Arab deputation went down to Egypt to see the Mufti of Jerusalem and demand the removal of his gangs; otherwise all the Arab inhabitants would evacuate Haifa, for they had not the hardihood to stand up to the Jews. The Mufti was unaccommodating.

In Jerusalem, our situation was bad. Before the establishment of the State Jerusalem was not a compact Jewish bloc; Jewish and Arab quarters were interspersed. For the Arabs the way to Jerusalem was open on four sides— from Ramallah on the north, Hebron on the south, Jericho on the east, and Jaffa-Latrun on the west. We had only one approach, from Tel Aviv-Latrun on the west. The Jews of the city needed food, and whereas supplies for Arab Jerusalem could be brought without difficulty from the neighboring villages, the Jewish villages in Galilee and in the valleys of Sharon, Jezreel, and Jordan were remote, and to convey food from them for hundreds of miles under fire became a vital operation in the defense of Jerusalem. The drivers of the convoys and their comrades on these runs, the boys and girls of Palmach, who together brought the harvests of the farms of Galilee and the valleys to the Jews of Jerusalem, wrote a noble chapter in our history.

Day after day, communications with the Capital became more difficult and dangerous. The principal British authorities, the High Commissioner included, had given us the clearest promises that freedom of movement would be maintained, but, like most promises given to us then, they were broken. The convoys going up to Jerusalem from Tel Aviv were attacked all along the road, and they had to stop when they entered the mountains and the risk mounted. Jerusalem was on the verge of famine.

Realizing that we must now go over to attack, I issued orders to the Hagana staff at the end of March, 1948, to collect a strong force and break through to Jerusalem. The staff met in my room and put forward a plan to organize a formation of four hundred men. No formation of that size had previously been committed to a single operation, but still I did not like the plan. It was only Jewish Jerusalem that was cut off from its hinterland; the Arab quarters were not. The Arabs well understood the importance of Jerusalem for us; they might lose the Old City without seriously prejudicing their position, but the destruction of Jewish Jerusalem could mean the end of the whole Yishuv. I knew that against our four hundred they could assemble four thousand and even more.

Insisting that the staff mobilize and commit at least fifteen hundred men, I was told, and correctly, that there were not that many to spare. Every man and every rifle had been dispatched to the various fronts throughout the country. I ascertained the number of armed men on each front and ordered that half their tally and half the tally of rifles be taken, excluding the Galilee.

The commanders were at once summoned to headquarters, and I gave them my personal instructions. Both the staff and the commanders accepted them enthusiastically and carried them out swiftly and loyally. The commanders displayed exemplary willingness, although each bore a heavy responsibility for the safety of the settlements in his zone. Galilee especially was in a perilous situation, and it was impossible to withdraw a single man; but even that area made its contribution of rifles.

Within a few hours the first Jewish offensive (called Operation Nachshon after the first of the Israelites to leap into the Red Sea in the exodus from Egypt) was organized, and it proved to be a turning point in the campaign. As if by a miracle, the first consignment of light machine guns arrived by air at a secret airfield the same night and was sent up to the Jerusalem front without an instant's delay. The way to Jerusalem was stormed, and Castel, the highest point, was occupied. In the battle for Castel, the Arab commander, Abdul Kader el-Husseini, was killed; both Arabs and British were dumbfounded by this sudden disclosure of Jewish striking power and morale.

In the four months following the United Nations resolution, despite continuing Arab attacks, not one of the enemy ever entered a Jewish settlement, though many of our villages were remote and sparsely inhabited. Not one settlement was destroyed, not one abandoned. In Haifa, Tel Aviv, and Jerusalem, Jews were forced to move from places near the border to buildings farther away because rifles, heavy machine guns, and mortars from the Arab side kept up a perpetual fusillade, but not one Jewish quarter was captured. Our forces, on the other hand, entered some villages that were miles from any

Jewish habitation, where the Arab bands were centered, even in the regions of Samaria and Judea, close to the Jordan border.

Arabs had begun to move out of the area set aside by the United Nations as a Jewish State, and long before the decisive battle for Haifa took place in the last week of April, a third of its Arab population had fled to Lebanon. Arabs left the mixed quarters in Jerusalem, and New Jerusalem became solidly Jewish; the Jews within the old Arab quarters held on, although under continuous attack.

As for the British, they did nothing to assist the implementation of the U.N. plan and very little to maintain a semblance of order in the country. In the Report of the Implementation Committee of Five, dated April 10, 1948, the attitude of the Mandatory power was summarized in these terms:

> The Commission could not change this position of the United Kingdom. It has had to accommodate itself to it and to negotiate with a view to adapting its plans for carrying on in Palestine after 15th May to the plans of the United Kingdom Government to abandon its responsibilities as a whole, while affording the successor authority no assistance which, in their view, would constitute implementation of the Assembly's resolution. The Palestine Administration has accordingly been unable to take any steps or to pursue any measures which would be designed to prepare the ground for the plan. This has been particularly serious in view of the inability of the Commission itself to be in Palestine. The refusal of the Mandatory Power to cooperate in implementing the plan, its rejection of any progressive transfer of authority and the inability of

the Commission to be in Palestine constitute a serious jeopardy to the discharge of the Commission's responsibilities.

According to the U.N. resolution, the British Mandate was to terminate "as soon as possible but in any case not later than August 1, 1948," by which date, also, British armed forces had been called upon to withdraw. In fact, the United Kingdom Government announced its intention of withdrawing on May 15. Meanwhile, it had allowed matters to go from bad to worse and had even paid little attention to the Security Council's appeal "to all Governments and people, particularly in and around Palestine, to take all possible action to prevent or reduce such disorders as are now occurring in Palestine."

On April 6 the Zionist General Council, the supreme body of the Movement in the periods between congresses, met in Tel Aviv, and there I made the following five proposals:

1. To call all our manpower to arms and to the settlements in the most rational manner possible and to the fullest extent that our defense needs dictate.

2. To prepare, manufacture, and procure the matériel we need, including all the means of land, sea, and air transport, in line with the preparations that have already been made and are now being made.

3. To organize our economy, industry, agriculture, commerce, export and import, and the distribution of food and raw materials on an emergency basis, so that we shall be able to maintain our growing military power and keep the Jewish economy going firmly under wartime conditions.

4. To set up in the Jewish community a single, su-

38

preme central authority to manage our manpower, command the armed forces, direct the labor force, supervise industry and agriculture, and run financial affairs and all the rest of our public services. This authority would have the full and loyal backing of the Zionist Movement and world Jewry.

5. Not to restrict ourselves to defense tactics but to attack, at the right time, all along the front, and not only in the territory designated for the Jewish State, not only within the borders of Palestine, but to strike at the enemy wherever he is to be found.

These proposals were accepted, and the Actions Committee decided to set up a National Administration of thirteen members which would become a Provisional Government on the day the State was proclaimed, and a National Council, which would become its provisional legislature.

The administration in Palestine was disintegrating but was still trying, whether directly or indirectly, to prevent, or at least to hinder, the Jewish community from defending itself. In opposition to the U.N. decision, the administration refused to vacate the port of Tel Aviv on February 7; although its police and army left the Tel Aviv area, British warships continued to cruise off its shores. There was, in fact, a sort of naval blockade along the coast of Palestine, directed against the Jewish community, for the frontiers were open to the Arabs to the north and the east and the south. Thousands of armed Arabs from across the borders, many of them army men and officers from the neighboring states, poured into Palestine, and their numbers were rapidly increasing. They came mainly from Syria, Iraq, and Trans-Jordan, and a few from Egypt as well. Many of them came carrying arms that had been sent to those countries by the British Government. The Arab Legion, too, was quartered in Palestine and it frequently participated in attacks on Jewish convoys. In the course of four months, ever since the first attack on November 30, over nine hundred Jews were killed. The Jews in the Old City of Jerusalem had already been besieged for several months, and even the New City had been half cut off throughout this period.

The British Government had announced that on May 15 the Mandate would come to an end and the administration and the army would leave the country—except that a British military force would remain in Haifa for some time longer. The public services were already breaking down, if not disappearing altogether, and on May 15 Palestine would lie open to total invasion by all the neighboring Arab states. The relation between the number of Jews in Palestine and the number of Arabs in the neighboring countries (not including North Africa) was about 1 to 45.

Under such conditions did our "National Administration" of thirteen members sit down to formulate the terms of that long-awaited and historic document, the Declaration of Independence.

There arose the question whether the Declaration ought to restrict itself to the framework of the United Nations decision or whether it should merely be based on the decision. The problem was whether to declare the State without specifying its borders or to specify the borders as fixed by the United Nations. I was opposed to specifying the borders. I pointed out that no borders were named in the American Declaration of Independence and maintained that we were under no obligation to designate them. To be sure, we had accepted the United Nations decision, but there was no telling whether the United Nations would back up its decision if we were attacked or intervene in the event that our neighbors attacked us and we defeated them. By a vote of 5-4 it was decided not to mention borders in the Declaration. A committee of five was appointed to draft the Declaration, which was approved, with some amendments, at a meeting of the National Administration on the morning of Friday, May 14.

We decided that the official declaration of the State would take place at four at a meeting of the National Council that afternoon in the Tel Aviv Museum, since Jerusalem was under siege and there was no possibility of our getting there that day. (At eleven that morning we learned that our four settlements in the Etzion bloc had been taken by the Arabs. The women, wounded, and noncombatants had been released and sent back to Jewish Jerusalem and the men taken prisoner.) About two hundred leaders of Palestine Jewry were invited to that festive occasion. The fact that the State was to be declared at this time was not publicized lest the heads of the British administration, scheduled to quit the country at midnight that night, decide to make some last-minute trouble. The members of the National Council and the rest of the nation's leaders who were in Jerusalem could not come, because Jerusalem was cut off. Only Rabbi Yehuda Leib Hacohen Maimon succeeded in getting to Tel Aviv, by Piper Cub. Present in the hall were the members of the Council in Tel Aviv, representatives of the World Zionist Organization and the Va'ad Leumi (the Jewish National Council which represented the Yishuv under the Mandate), literary and artistic figures, journalists, party leaders, the chief rabbis, the Hagana Chief of Staff and his colleagues, and representatives of the community's economic bodies.

Yet, news of the declaration spread among the public, who poured into the streets, especially near the Museum, carrying flags of blue and white, which had become the official colors of the State about to be born.

Two hours before the declaration, there was a joint meeting with the Hagana General Staff, at which Yigael Yadin, Chief of Operations, said that according to his information the armies of five Arab states—Egypt, Jordan, Iraq, Syria, and Lebanon—equipped with tanks, warplanes, and light arms, stood poised to invade the country at midnight, as soon as the High Commissioner left and the Mandate ended.

With heavy heart I set out a few minutes before four for the Museum to proclaim the establishment of the Jewish State, which we had decided to name "Israel." When I arrived the auditorium was full. The streets were jammed with throngs keyed up and elated.

Inside the auditorium, behind the dais, hung a huge photograph of Theodore Herzl. The Philharmonic Orchestra played "Hatikva," which had been made the new State's national anthem. Then I held in my hands the Declaration, which I read with a heart filled at once with trepidation and exaltation. I tried to overcome my emotion and read the Declaration in a loud, clear tone, as everybody rose to hear it. Rabbi Maimon, the *doyen* of us all, recited the blessing thanking the Almighty for "sustaining us so that we have lived to see this day." I informed the assembly that the members of the National Council in Jerusalem who, regrettably, could not be present had met at Jewish Agency headquarters and notified us that all of them joined in the Declaration.

42

Then I read the first manifesto of the Council, which by virtue of the Declaration of Independence had become the Provisional Council of State. The manifesto stated:

1. The Provisional Council of State (with 34 members) is the highest legislative organ of the State of Israel. The Provisional Council of State has the right to delegate part of its authority to the Provisional Government for the purpose of enacting urgent legislation.
2. All legislation resulting from the White Paper of 1939 is null and void.
3. The land transfer regulations of 1940 are hereby nullified retroactively to May 18, 1939.
4. Until other legislation is enacted by the legislative organs of our State, the legal system prevailing on May 14, 1948, will remain in force.

I then signed my name at the end of the Declaration and asked my colleagues in the Council to come up to the dais and sign in alphabetical order. Spaces in the same order were reserved for our colleagues in Jerusalem. Everybody present signed, I announced that the State of Israel was now in existence, and the meeting was adjourned.

In the streets the throngs sang and danced. I proceeded directly to General Staff headquarters. In my diary I wrote that day: "At four o'clock in the afternoon Jewish independence was declared and the State of Israel was established. Its destiny is now in the hands of our defense forces."

At Staff headquarters disturbing reports had arrived of large enemy concentrations all along the southern, eastern, and northern borders. Long convoys of Arab armor were moving down all the roads.

At midnight the High Commissioner, Sir Alan Cunningham, left, and the Arab invasion began. I returned immediately to Command headquarters.

Just before dawn, I broadcast to America from the Hagana station in Tel Aviv, which now emerged from underground and became the official broadcasting station of the Israel security forces (the Israel Defense Forces did not yet exist, for the ordinance creating them was only published on May 26). In my broadcast I dwelt briefly on the course of our struggle since the U.N. resolution of November 29, 1947, the declaration of war on Israel by the Arab states, members of the United Nations, in defiance of United Nations authority, the dangers awaiting us, and our readiness to resist, even if we were attacked on land, at sea, and in the air. While I was speaking, the first bombs were dropped by Egyptian planes not far from the broadcasting station at Mahane Yona. The noise was earsplitting, but I was used to it from the period of the blitz in London, and I concluded my talk calmly, telling my listeners that Tel Aviv was being bombed at that moment by Egyptian planes.

When I had finished, I hurried over to the scene of the damage. The Tel Aviv airfield and the Reading power station had been the targets of the enemy's first bombing expedition. One hangar was in flames, several wounded had been taken to hospital, and a few of our planes had been put out of service.

From the airfield I went home, and on the way I saw the faces of Tel Avivians peering from all the windows. The sun was just rising. There was concern in their faces, but no sign of panic or fear, and I knew in my heart that these people would stand their ground.

Chapter Three
Israel's First Steps

On May 19 I was able to inform the Provisional State Council:

At the moment the enemy controls the air. Everybody sitting here knows exactly what that means for Tel Aviv. There are grounds for assuming that this situation will not continue for long; to my regret I cannot specify the deadline. Control of the air gives the enemy a considerable advantage, but our people are not panicking. The Yishuv is not in need of compliments, but we cannot let its glorious stand pass unnoticed. I went through the Nazi blitz in London, and I was filled with wonder at the supreme heroism which the people of London displayed during the terrible days of incessant air attack. But our people are not made of lesser stuff than the people of London.

On June 3 I was able to inform the Council:

There is still cause for concern about the future. But we can look back on the immediate past with more than a little satisfaction. Considering the short time that has passed since the termination of the Mandate and the military and political goals the invading countries set themselves, they may be said to have been routed politically and soundly trounced militarily. Their plan to settle the fate of the State of Israel with a quick invasion from the north, the east and the west, with heavy equipment, has been pricked like a bubble. The State of Israel still stands; the invaders are further from conquest and victory than they were three weeks ago. The Israeli armies today hold more contiguous territory than they did three weeks ago. Our armies now control all the territory designated for the Jewish State by the United Nations, as well as several important areas outside this territory. The latter include Western Galilee and almost the entire Tel Aviv-Jerusalem road, except for two small but crucial stretches, where travel is still hazardous: the flanks of the road from Sha'ar Hagai to Jerusalem, and several points along the road in the Shefela. Nearly all of New Jerusalem is in our hands. But we cannot ignore the heavy losses we have suffered in this sector. After an heroic stand, which will forever occupy a prominent place in the annals of Jewish valor and the history of the Jewish people, the Etzion bloc fell. And the Jewish community of the Old City, after holding out valiantly for a month, fell to the hosts of the Arab Legion on May 28. This is the heaviest blow we have suffered at the hands of the Arabs.

On May 26 the Provisional Government had empowered me to issue an order proclaiming the establishment

46

of the Israel Defense Forces. On May 31, 1948, I had issued an order of the day declaring:

> With the establishment of the State of Israel the Hagana has left the underground and become a regular army.
>
> The Yishuv and the Jewish people owe a great debt to the Hagana, from its inception and the fulfillment of its first tasks in Petah Tikva, Rishon LeZion, Gedera, Rosh Pina, Zichron Ya'akov, and Metulla, through Hashomer of the Second Aliya period, the Jewish Legion of World War I, the defenders of Tel Hai, the steady growth of the national defense organization in the period between the two World Wars, the Jewish Settlement Police during the disturbances of 1936-39, the Palmach, the field forces, the mass enlistment during World War II, and the first Jewish brigade, up to the tremendous showing the Hagana made in the first half of the war against us between November 30, 1947 and May 31, 1948.
>
> Without the experience, the planning, the capacity to act, command, and obey, the loyalty and valor, of the Hagana, the Yishuv would not have survived the terrible ordeal of blood it went through during these six months and we would not have achieved the State of Israel. In the chronicles of the Jewish people, the Hagana chapter will shine with a grandeur and glory that shall never be dimmed.
>
> Now a new chapter is beginning—the regular army of the State of Israel is being established, the army of Jewish freedom and sovereignty in our Homeland. . . .

A truce was arranged by the United Nations and came into force on June 11, almost exactly one month after the

Arab invasion had begun. The truce was an uneasy affair, and on July 9 war was resumed. Deliveries of military equipment, and of a few aircraft, which we had long awaited, had been made during the period of the truce, and we were in a better position *vis-à-vis* our enemies at the end of the truce than when it began. There were ten days of sharp fighting, during which our forces took Lydda airport and the town of Ramleh, on the road to Jerusalem, captured Nazareth in Galilee, and broadened the corridor we had already opened between Jerusalem and the coast.

The second truce began on July 19, but although our forces had been conspicuously successful in all other areas, a powerful Egyptian army was still holding vital areas of the Negev, which had been awarded to Israel in the U.N. Partition Plan and which, although mainly barren and waterless, I regarded as an essential area of settlement and communications (touching as it does upon the Red Sea), as well as strategically indispensable. The Egyptian occupation of this territory had cut off several of our agricultural settlements. By the truce arrangements, we were given the right to convey food supplies to these isolated communities; the Egyptians, however, ignored the agreement and we therefore decided to force them back upon the sea and Sinai.

We called the plan Operation Ten Plagues, after the afflictions that fell upon Egypt after Pharaoh refused to let the Israelites go. Our operation began on October 14. Beersheba was captured, and within a week we had the Egyptians in full retreat, except for a small pocket of Sudanese at Faluja, in the northern Negev.

The Egyptian army withdrew to a strip of territory against the sea at Gaza, which was backed by the main Egyptian base at El Arish, on the coast of Sinai. Operation Ten Plagues, which had been brilliantly successful, was followed by a daring plunge into Sinai itself, the object of which was to cripple the Egyptian army and so insure the safety of the southern borders at least for a few years. Our forces, well ahead of schedule and deep into Sinai, were on the point of accomplishing their objective when, at the request of the President of the United States, transmitted to me by his Ambassador, James McDonald, I ordered that the operation be broken off and that our forces be withdrawn immediately from the Sinai Peninsula.

Meanwhile, the Egyptians had asked for an armistice.

Victory in the War of Independence, glorious as it was, cost us five thousand and more of our most precious lives. No tributes, no sympathy, can make good their loss to the bereaved, but I believe, truly and simply, that if ever Jewish lives were not lost in vain since the revolt of the Maccabees, it was then.

The War of Independence was a crossroad in Israel's history, as significant as the wars of Joshua, son of Nun, or the campaigns of the Hasmoneans. It was not a sudden leap from nothingness, any more than the State of Israel, whose proclamation ushered in a new era in the life of the Land and the people, sprang up out of the void. The State had its origin not in that proclamation but in the hazardous labors of settlement undertaken by three generations of pioneers. The State was a new link in the chain of history for which we had waited 1,835 years, since the defeat of Bar-Kochba, the leader of the last Jewish revolt against the Romans.

The Israel Defense Forces were not just a continuation of the Hagana but a completely new revelation of the sovereign power of the Hebrews after the royal days of Judah and Israel.

By the end of that fateful year, 1948, which had seen the rebirth of the sovereign Land of Israel and the supreme testing of its people in war, we had regained all the territory allotted to us under the 1947 U.N. Partition Resolution and had added roughly one-third.

The armistice negotiations took place on the Greek island of Rhodes and were conducted under the supervision of that remarkable man, Dr. Ralph Bunche. The first Armistice Agreement was concluded with Egypt and was signed on February 24, 1949; the second, with Lebanon, was signed on March 23; the third, with Jordan, on April 3; and the fourth, with Syria, on July 29. Iraq refused to negotiate.

The Armistice Agreements begin with the following words: "With a view to promoting the return of permanent peace in Palestine . . . , the following principles . . . are hereby affirmed. . . ." Some of the main principles, common to all four agreements, were formulated as follows:

No aggressive action by the armed forces—land, sea, or air—of either Party shall be undertaken, planned, or threatened against the people or the armed forces of the other; . . . (Article I, paragraph 2)

No element of the land, sea, or air military or paramilitary forces of either Party, including non-regular forces, shall commit any warlike or hostile act against the military or para-military forces of the other Party, or against civilians in territory under the control of that Party; . . . (Article II, paragraph 2)

After this Agreement has been in effect for one year from the date of its signing, either of the Parties may call upon the Secretary-General of the United Nations

50

to convoke a conference of representatives of the two Parties for the purpose of reviewing, revising, or suspending any of the provisions of this Agreement other than Articles I and II. (Article XII)

The Arab rulers, however, would not reconcile themselves to the existence of Israel, and after they had failed to crush us by force of arms they launched a program of trying to undermine our existence by economic and political means, as well as by force, where possible.

The Arab League (Egypt, Trans-Jordan, Syria, Lebanon, Iraq, Saudi Arabia, and Yemen), established by the inspiration of the British before the rise of the State of Israel, now organized an economic boycott against Israel and against every company anywhere that maintained trade and economic ties with us. To prevent new settlements from flourishing, and to discourage the establishment of others, the Arabs organized terrorism, murder, and sabotage wherever possible. Insofar as it lay within their power, they brought pressure to bear on the governments of a number of countries to close the gates of exit to Jews who wanted to emigrate. Preparations for a second round under a unified command were begun.

It is the duty of the United Nations Organization to preserve the peace and security of its members and of the entire world, to adopt collective measures to prevent threats to peace, and to suppress every act of aggression or other breach of the peace.

The first article of the United Nations Charter lays down the aims of the Organization as follows:

1. To maintain international peace and security, and to that end: to take effective collective measures for the prevention and removal of threats to the peace,

and for the suppression of acts of aggression or other breaches of the peace, and to bring about by peaceful means, and in conformity with the principles of justice and international law, adjustment or settlement of international disputes or situations which might lead to a breach of the peace;

2. To develop friendly relations among nations based on respect for the principle of equal rights and self-determination of peoples, and to take other appropriate measures to strengthen universal peace;

3. To achieve international cooperation in solving international problems of an economic, social, cultural or humanitarian character. . . .

But the United Nations did not do its duty when the Arab countries attacked the State of Israel immediately after it was established, nor did the organization lift a finger throughout the years when the Arabs were violating their obligations under the United Nations Charter. Article 2 of the Charter obligates the organization and its members, in pursuance of the aims laid down in the Charter, to act in accordance with these principles:

1. The Organization is based on the principle of the sovereign equality of all its Members.

2. All Members shall settle their international disputes by peaceful means in such a manner that international peace and security, and justice, are not endangered.

3. All Members shall refrain in their international relations from the threat or use of force against the territorial integrity or political independence of any state, or in any other manner inconsistent with the Purposes of the United Nations.

Of all the neighboring countries that signed armistice agreements with Israel and undertook, as members of the United Nations, to fulfill the obligations contained in the Charter, Egypt has done the most to violate international law, the principles of the United Nations, and its Armistice Agreement with Israel.

In spite of the stupendous tasks it faced and the unremitting threats of its Arab neighbors, the State of Israel from the beginning had to organize its civil structure simultaneously with its defense structure. For one thing, we had come into existence as a state not merely to give freedom and independence to the 650,000 Jews who were its citizens on May 14, 1948, but also and above all to create a sovereign Homeland for all Jews waiting outside. It was our immediate responsibility to see that the Homeland should be organized in accordance with modern democratic principles and that the entry of the newcomers into the land that was as much theirs as ours should at least have the basis and promise of reasonable social and economic conditions.

These matters had not been made easier for us by the British Mandatory regime's refusal to recognize any successor authority or to hand over to us, through the U.N. if need be, the machinery of government. Fortunately, we were fairly well organized through the Jewish Agency and the Va'ad Leumi (the Jewish National Council, representing the Jews of Palestine), and had at least the nucleus of a national administration.

Owing, however, to the compelling pressure of the War of Independence, we were still without a properly elected government at the end of 1948. Early in January, 1949, we resolved upon general elections and, although still at war in the south, set the date at January 25. Meanwhile, Egypt had asked for armistice negotiations and our people had gained more confidence in the future. The Provisional Government had decided upon a unicameral parliament of 120 members to be elected by proportional representation.

The general elections were held peacefully on January 25. The first Knesset of the State of Israel, meeting for the occasion in the auditorium of the Jewish Agency building in Jerusalem, on February 16 elected Dr. Chaim Weizmann first President of the State. Eleven political parties were represented, elected under universal suffrage according to the list system. My own party, Mapai, roughly equivalent to the British Labor party, had polled 35.7 per cent of the votes and was therefore entitled to 46 seats. It was by far the largest group in the Knesset and I was entrusted with the task of forming a coalition government, of which I became Prime Minister and Minister of Defense.

Jerusalem was by decree of our history our Capital, but, for the time being, the first Knesset decided to meet in an unoccupied cinema theater on the seafront of Tel Aviv.

Our people had defended their part of Jerusalem with their lives and we had no intention of surrendering it to an international or any other regime. The U.N. plan, although it still exists in theory, ceased to have any practical meaning. Almost from the beginning, the majority of the member states recognized the Arab half of Jerusalem as *de facto* Arab territory within the Hashemite Kingdom of Jordan, and the Jewish half as *de facto* Israel territory subject to the authority of the Government of the State of Israel.

At the end of 1949 the United Nations General Assembly resumed discussion of the Jerusalem problem and decided that the city should be under United Nations jurisdiction, in order to protect and to preserve the unique spiritual and religious interests located in the city of the three great monotheistic faiths throughout the world, Christian, Jewish, and Moslem. On December 5, 1949, following this decision, I told the Knesset:

Israel is a member of the United Nations, not for reasons of political convenience, but out of deep and traditional regard for the ideals of universal peace and the brotherhood of man which the prophets have bequeathed to us—and which the United Nations Organization has emblazoned on its standard.

Our membership obliges us to proclaim here, on the platform of Israel's First Knesset, for the benefit of all the nations gathered together in the United Nations General Assembly and all who cherish peace and justice, what the feelings of the Jewish people have been about its holy city Jerusalem, since it first became a nation united under the scepter of King David three thousand years ago, and what our attitude is to the holy places of all religions.

In proclaiming the re-establishment of Jewish national sovereignty in the State of Israel on May 14, 1948, we declared and undertook before history and the world that "the State of Israel will guarantee freedom of religion, conscience, language, education and culture; will protect the holy places of all religions, and will be faithful to the principles of the United Nations Charter."

Accordingly, our delegation to the United Nations has announced that Israel undertakes to respect all existing rights regarding the holy places and religious buildings in Jerusalem, promises freedom of worship and free access without discrimination to all the holy places and religious buildings under its control, recognizes the right of pilgrims of all nations and religions to visit the holy places in Israel, as well as freedom of movement to clergymen, and, furthermore, that it agrees to the maintenance by the U.N. of effective supervision of the holy places and of the existing rights, under an agreement to be reached between the United Nations and Israel.

At the same time, we consider ourselves duty-bound to declare that Jewish Jerusalem is an organic and inseparable part of the State of Israel, just as it is an inseparable part of Jewish history, Jewish religion, and the Jewish soul. Jerusalem is the very heart of the State of Israel. We are proud that Jerusalem is also considered sacred by members of other religions, and we shall gladly guarantee them the greatest possible freedom and help in satisfying their religious needs in Jerusalem. We shall also give the United Nations every assistance toward this end.

But we cannot conceive that the United Nations Organization will try to sever Jerusalem from the State of Israel or to impair Israel's sovereignty—in Israel's Eternal Capital.

I then proposed to the Cabinet that the Knesset and the ministries (except the Ministry of Defense) be moved to Jerusalem. On December 13, 1949, I told the Knesset:

We respect and shall continue to respect the wishes of all states concerned for freedom of worship and free access to the holy places, and which wish to safeguard the existing rights with respect to holy places and religious buildings in Jerusalem. We stand by our undertaking to preserve these rights and we shall gladly fulfill it, although we shall not be party to the forced severance of Jerusalem, which would be an unwarranted and unjustifiable violation of the historic and natural right of the Jewish people in their ancestral Homeland.

Meanwhile, Jewish immigrants had been pouring in at an unprecedented rate. A few weeks before the transfer of the Knesset to the Capital, our Jewish population had reached a million; it had grown by 350,000 in a year and a half, almost entirely by immigration. The influx continued undiminished, and by May, 1952, another 350,000 had come; the number of Jews in Israel had doubled within four years.

The problems faced by our newly established Government departments, notably those of Labor (responsible for housing), Health, Education, Trade and Industry, as well as the relevant departments of the Jewish Agency, were complex, and it is understandable that there should have been severe criticism in some quarters. However, despite grave shortages of foodstuffs and other commodities, which had compelled us to impose a severe austerity program, and despite security threats and murderous Arab raiding in the border areas, we kept the gates wide open, even encouraging a flood of newcomers unlike anything since the days of Joshua.

Of the 700,000 new Israelis who had been added within four years to the 650,000 Jews in the country when the State was proclaimed, more than 300,000 survivors of the concentration camps came from displaced persons' camps and eastern Europe. Those who, defying the Mandatory Government's blockade, had been waylaid by British naval patrols as they tried to reach the Homeland and carried off to camps in Cyprus were released by the British authorities when the Mandate ended and were at once brought to Haifa and Tel Aviv, although these ports were being bombed at the time by enemy aircraft.

Almost 250,000 of the new immigrants came from the Asian countries—Iraq, Iran, Turkey, Yemen, India, and Aden. When tidings of the new state reached the ancient Jewry of Yemen, they left in a body—45,000 men, women, and children—and braved the perils of an uncharted desert to reach sanctuary here.

There were Jewish communities, hundreds of years old and rooted deep in their adopted countries, which began to pack up and make their way to Israel. The first was the Jewry of Bulgaria: 40,000 out of 45,000 members emigrated. Of Libya's 35,000 Jews all but 3,000 came, most of them in the first year of the State.

No sooner had the last contingents from Poland arrived than thousands of immigrants began to come from Rumania. And before Rumanian immigration stopped, Operation Babylon, the exodus from Iraq, began. Jews had started to arrive from that country in June, 1950, but only in 1951 did the pace of their entry quicken. The Iraqi Government seized all the property of those who left, and most of them arrived nearly destitute. Some 120,000 immigrants in all came from Iraq.

With the backing of world Jewry, and the help given us by the United States Government, we were able to start building the temporary quarters needed for the new arrivals. Known in Hebrew as *ma'barot* (sing. *ma'bara*), these were a form of transit camp—far from satisfactory but the best we could do at that time.

There is no doubt that the immigrants found life very hard in the *ma'barot*, where in many ways they had to fend for themselves, and the winter of 1951 was exceptionally severe. We started a network of Hebrew schools for adults, which helped many of the immigrants to leave their temporary quarters more quickly and become absorbed in the economy of the country. However, the *ma'barot* offered only an immediate solution to the housing problem; we never lost sight of their temporary nature, and nothing was left undone to raise the means to build permanent dwellings.

The housing of these newcomers, the care they had to be given until such time as we could begin to integrate them into the social and economic life of the country, the attention that had to be paid to their health, the need to give them a grounding in the Hebrew language, the training of the adults in agriculture or industry or some appropriate craft, and often in the elementary upbringing of their children—these represented an enormous undertaking.

However, we could not be persuaded to put any restrictions on immigration. The State of Israel had been brought into being to provide, as of right, a home for these people. From an economic and even social point of view, it might have been more practical to reduce the pace of immigration, but immigration was not only an urgent question of security (as it is today), but a redemption of Jews from spiritual and possibly physical extinction in the Diaspora.

On July 3, 1950, I introduced in the Knesset the Law of the Return, which as I told the House at the time, embodies a central mission of our State: the ingathering of the exiles. This law declares that the State does not confer on any Jew outside the right to settle in Israel; this right is inherent in his very Jewishness and is his to exercise at his own free will. Israeli Jews are not privileged above non-Jews. The State is based on the absolute equality of all its citizens in rights and duties. This principle is clearly enunciated in the Declaration of Independence, which promises that Israel will maintain complete equality of social and political rights for all its citizens without distinction of creed, race, or sex. But it is not the State that confers on Diaspora Jews the right to return. This right is older than the State of Israel; in fact, it is this right that built the State. It derives from the uninterrupted historical link between the Jewish people and their ancestral Homeland, a link which the law of nations has also recognized.

Every Jew everywhere has the historical right to return to and settle in Israel, whether because he feels himself to be a second-class citizen where he is, or because he feels insecure about his survival, or because he is oppressed, or because he is surrounded by hate and scorn, or because he cannot live the kind of Jewish life he wishes to live, or because of his love of his time-honored traditions, Hebrew culture, and Jewish national sovereignty.

Israel can have no real security without immigration. The population of Egypt alone numbers twenty-six millions. Israel's population in 1952 was something over one million, and even today it is only some two million. Aliya means not only bringing Jews to Israel's shores. It also means enabling the immigrant to take root in the soil of the Homeland and its independent economy, in the Hebrew language, in the nation's values and spiritual heritage; imbuing him with national pride and confidence, the will and capacity to build and defend the Homeland, and to mold a new society, based on freedom, social justice, and co-operation.

Security means the settlement and peopling of the

empty areas in our north and south, the dispersal of the population and the establishment of industries throughout the country, the development of agriculture in all suitable areas, and the building of an expanding economy that will provide our people with a livelihood and liberate them from dependence on material aid from outside. It has always been my profound conviction that these developments are imperative for our survival.

In the anxious days following our victory in the War of Independence, I had no doubt that the ambitious Arab rulers, dependent on spectacular promise and emotional bluster for their prestige rather than upon good government and expanding social welfare, would continually be tempted to wage war against us. Close settlement of our land, dispersal of the population, and rapid development of our economy were continuing security imperatives.

In those early years it was also clear that security meant the conquest of the sea and the air as well as the soil. Israel had to become an important maritime power; the economic boycott by the Arab states and the blockading of the Suez Canal by Egypt only emphasized this need. In ancient, medieval, and modern times small peoples, living by the sea, have become great maritime powers by the development of shipping and fisheries. The first historic example was given by men living in our own country and speaking Hebrew as we did: the peoples of Tyre and Sidon. The prophet Ezekiel has left us an impressive account of the greatness and power of Tyre, "that dwelleth at the entry of the sea, that is the merchant of the peoples unto many isles." As a security objective, therefore, as well as within the framework of our plans for general economic expansion, we began in those days

61

to train a large part of our youth, and those new immigrants who had appropriate qualifications and an interest in seacraft, in sea fishing and ocean shipping.

In addition, security meant, of course, defense forces. We could not hope to equal numerically the forces of our avowed enemies, or match the quantity of their armaments, but we had to achieve a qualitative balance in both.

Such were the heavy responsibilities of the State of Israel and its first formal Government, as they have been of every succeeding Government.

Israel's first days were stimulating, and I was but one member of a hard-working, fervent Cabinet. Holding the office of Prime Minister, I was hardly less occupied with my portfolio of Defense. I felt a profound affection for the army, born in the perilous days of invasion, which had saved our people, upheld our independence, and, by these deeds, laid the foundations of our supreme undertaking—the ingathering of the exiles.

There was much yet to be done in all fields of endeavor, and first and foremost it was necessary to make a huge capital outlay, for which we had not adequate means. To assist in obtaining those resources, we launched a State of Israel Bond drive in the United States, and in May, 1951, on the eve of our third anniversary as a State, I flew to America to explain our situation and emphasize our needs.

Long shall I remember the moving welcome given me by President Truman and the people of the United States. I toured the country from end to end, telling about Israel and learning about America. Then, after four exhilarating weeks, I returned to Israel.

Gradually, our little State showed signs of prospering,

and of a development that gave promise of economic independence within a foreseeable future. More irrigation projects could be undertaken to bring back life to areas barren after centuries of neglect; industries began to spring up, providing work and creating an export trade; our merchant fleet was steadily expanded and the flag of Israel began to appear in the ports of Europe, the Americas, and Asia. Housing conditions steadily improved and we were able to relax our austerity program as more and more food was produced from our own soil, and more and more products, including industrial goods, were exported.

Such achievements were unfortunately only a part of the picture. Murderous raids from the Egyptian-held Gaza Strip were increasing and were beginning to catch up in frequency with those from Jordan. In 1951 the Security Council rejected as incompatible with the Armistice Agreement Egypt's claim that a state of belligerency existed, and ruled that Egypt was therefore not entitled to deny Israel freedom of passage through the Suez Canal. Egypt repudiated the Council's ruling—but there was no effective United Nations reaction. To make matters worse, Egypt, which in 1950 had seized the uninhabited islands of Tiran and Sanafir near the Red Sea entrance to the Gulf of Aqaba, had set up a powerful garrison at Sharm el-Sheikh, on the Egyptian mainland close to the two islands, and was obstructing Israeli navigation through the straits to and from our port of Eilat. Just as the United Nations had done nothing to compel Egypt to conform to its ruling on the subject of Israel's right of passage through the Suez Canal, so the United States, which had received from the Egyptian Government an express undertaking that occupation of the two islands was not intended to obstruct navigation in the Straits of Tiran, did nothing to insure that this undertaking would be respected.

For the time being we had to leave the situation as it was. We were in no position, by ourselves, to compel Egypt to open the Suez Canal to our ships or to remove her forces from their positions at the entrance to the Gulf of Aqaba. For a brief period I had hopes of some change of policy in Cairo. In August, 1952, a military coup took place in Egypt and a group of officers under the leadership of Mohammed Naguib succeeded in dethroning King Farouk and assuming power. On August 18, 1952, I told Parliament:

> Apart from two strong and stable states in the Middle East, Israel and Turkey, all the Middle Eastern countries are in a whirlpool of unrest, breeding revolt, political chaos, assassination, dethronement of kings, and constant competition for power between adventurous dictators. In this confused and disturbed atmosphere, a spark struck in any corner may kindle a blaze of unpredictable intensity and size, and we shall be endangering our very existence if we are not alert and prepared for any eventuality.
>
> It may be that in the midst of this tempestuous development there are also positive tendencies of reform and progress. Wherever such tendencies exist, we regard them with favor. The events that have taken place in Egypt during the past few weeks should be welcomed, and we are prepared to accept the testimony of Mohammed Naguib that he and most of his colleagues in the Egyptian army were opposed to the invasion of Israel and that Farouk was mainly responsible for it. It may be that their reasons for opposing it

were purely military, but there is no doubt that there was not at the time, and there is not now, any cause or basis for strife between Israel and Egypt. The two countries are separated by a broad and extensive desert, and there is therefore no room for border disputes; there was not, nor is there now, any reason for political, economic, or territorial antagonism between the two neighbors.

Israel wishes to see a free, independent, and progressive Egypt. We bear her no ill will for what she did to our forefathers in the days of Pharaoh or to ourselves four years ago. Despite the headstrong behavior of Farouk's government toward us, we demonstrated good will toward her in the months of her involvement with a Great Power and did not think of exploiting the occasion to attack, as she did when our State was established, or to be revenged upon her.

But we cannot ignore the fact that even this Egypt shows no sign of readiness to repair the grievous wrong committed by the deposed King Farouk, and none of us can see with certainty in which direction Egypt's face is turned: toward peace or war.

Mohammed Naguib did not last long as head of the revolution. A younger officer, Gamal Abdel Nasser, deposed him and, with the aid of other young officers, gained complete control over Egypt. In a pamphlet called *The Philosophy of the Revolution,* this young dictator gave a frank and open account of his political ambitions. He laid down three objectives: (1) to gain power over all the Arab countries, (2) to become the head of all the Moslem peoples, and (3) to become the leader of the entire African continent.

The internal reforms for whose sake the revolution had

ostensibly been carried out—the improvement of the nation's health, popular education, the development of resources, and the raising of material standards—were apparently deferred to the distant future and replaced by political ambitions. Constructive reforms to improve the conditions of the people require patience, perseverance, prolonged effort, opposition to the great landowners, making demands on the people itself; but it is in the nature of dictatorships that they are eager for easy and rapid victories, and the new rulers of Egypt believed that it would be easier to achieve intoxicating victories in the field of foreign policy than to rectify the wretched and shameful situation at home.

Nasser, apparently, came to the conclusion that the least difficult and costly method of gaining hegemony of the Arab world was to strike at Israel. Specially trained gangs of marauders, called *fedayun,* based in the Gaza Strip, were ordered to cross Israel's borders to commit acts of terrorism and sabotage.

Thus were our problems of security and settlement interlocked. Toward the end of 1953, I had the impression that these problems might well become highly critical in the course of a year or two. At the same time, I was disturbed by the evidence of more and more new immigrants settling in already overcrowded cities and towns instead of moving out into the empty lands of the Negev and Galilee. No doubt our Arab neighbors, who as a matter of policy wanted to create conditions of insecurity in these open areas and along our borders, were pleased. The more I saw of this trend, the stronger was the temptation I felt to go out into our wilderness and be among those who were making that wilderness fruitful. In addition, I was feeling the strain of the pressure I had been under since May, 1948.

I therefore informed the Central Committee of my party, Mapai, that I had decided to retire from the Cabinet, although I would retain my seat in the Knesset. The decision met with opposition and some consternation, but I was resolved not to change my mind. The newspapers vied with each other in posing possible reasons for my decision. On November 2, 1953, I submitted my resignation to President Ben-Zvi, who had succeeded Dr. Chaim Weizmann after the latter's death, on November 9, 1952. In my letter of resignation I stated that no one man is indispensable to the government of a country, and that I most certainly was not. Lawful government is maintained though prime ministers come and go, and I had no reason to suppose that my departure would cause a crisis. My friend Moshe Sharett, Minister for Foreign Affairs, had been appointed acting Prime Minister and I was confident that a new government would be formed and approved by the Knesset without undue delay or upheaval.

That evening, broadcasting to the nation, I summarized some, at least, of the motives impelling me to take leave of the Government, with a paraphrase of the words of the prophet Habakkuk: "But the righteous shall live by his faith" (Habakkuk 2:4). He will not preach to others or act the saint by calling on others to live justly; he will not look for fault in his neighbor, but will practice his faith in his daily life; he will live it.

On Sunday, December 13, my wife and I left our home for a small settlement in the Negev called Sdeh Boker, which had been founded on May 15, 1952, by young men and women who had done military service in the Negev and were now raising sheep on the lean pastures of this almost rainless land.

Chapter Four
The Storm Clouds Gather

Early in 1955, my good friend and colleague of long standing, Golda Myerson (Meir), at that time Minister of Labor in Moshe Sharett's Government, came down to see me at Sdeh Boker. The border situation had been steadily deteriorating, and the security risks were mounting, as Nasser and other Arab leaders began concentrating on the expansion and rearmament of their already considerable armies.

Golda Myerson and I examined these various problems. She conveyed to me the request of the Prime Minister, Moshe Sharett, that I should re-enter active politics and return to the post of Minister of Defense, as grave difficulties had arisen in the Ministry and all my friends urged my return to the Government. I proposed one of my friends who had for many years had the confidence of the Hagana. But when he declined and insisted on my coming back in view of the grave security situation, I accepted Sharett's invitation and a few days later went back to Jerusalem, soon afterwards taking my place again in the familiar whitewashed office of the Ministry of Defense. The general elections were held in July, following which I became, once again, Prime Minister, in a coalition headed by my own party, Mapai, and including Mizrahi (later the National Religious party), the left-wing Achdut Ha'avoda (Unity of Labor), Mapam (United Workers), from which Achdut Ha'avoda had earlier split off, and the Progressive party, a non-Socialist liberal group.

Although there were differences among us in our conceptions of the nature of the state we were trying to mold in Israel, one thing, I knew, was common ground, however we might diverge on social, economic, and cultural issues: *we must survive in our land.* Security had to be the pivotal point of any policy. For us it was not merely a matter of safeguarding our independence and territory, our frontiers and our way of government; it was a matter of sheer physical survival. Our adversary was making ready, as many Arab leaders publicly avowed, to hurl us into the sea. Shocked by the prodigal supply of arms flowing to the Arab countries, especially Egypt, we knew that our defense required more than an army with weapons of war. The people, with their sound instinct, realized that to achieve security we had to fortify ourselves with spiritual as well as military weapons. The new Government was to become a Government of crisis from the very start.

Shortly before November, 1955, we received the grave news of the "deal" between Czechoslovakia and Egypt whereby the former would supply Nasser with enormous quantities of modern arms of the best quality. With one stroke our security situation was entirely changed. The Government of Czechoslovakia called it a "commercial transaction," and there is no point in arguing about the term. Selling poison to a known murderer may be described in the same way. I had too much respect for the political understanding and realism of the Czech Government not to be certain that it knew perfectly well the purpose of the great consignments of tanks, planes, guns, submarines, and other equipment that it was delivering to Egypt. It knew as well as I that these arms would not be used to improve the living conditions of the Egyptian workers and *fellahin,* to stamp out widespread disease, or to eradicate illiteracy. It knew that Nasser was buying arms for one purpose, and one only: to destroy Israel and her people.

The Czech Government had no doubt heard the recurring Arab threats of a second round and was surely not so naïve as its official organ, *Rude Pravo,* which proclaimed that "the peace-loving policy of the Arab countries is known to all." The views of those who rule in Cairo are voiced by the newspapers there and not in Prague, and the opinion voiced by the Egyptian press was unequivocal: "The Arabs regard Israel as an artificial state which must be destroyed." Radio Cairo was just as outspoken. The Egyptian Foreign Minister sought to persuade opinion in America that what Radio Cairo said was not official; but under a military dictatorship broadcasts are controlled and no statement can be made without official consent. Radio Cairo could boast at the end of 1955: "The day of Israel's destruction approaches. This is our decision and this is our faith. There shall be no peace on the borders, for we demand vengeance, and vengeance means death to Israel."

The Czech Government could not fail to realize that the shipments of arms to Egypt were likely to kindle a terrible conflagration in the Middle East, but it turned a deaf ear to the flow of Nazi dogma that came from Cairo.

We knew that it acted with the knowledge, and perhaps the prompting, of the Soviet Union. We had already made known our case to the representative of the Soviet Union, Mr. Molotov, at the Geneva meeting of the Big Four in late October, 1955, but had received no satisfactory reply.

In 1950, England, France and the United States had signed a tripartite declaration in which they agreed to maintain a balance of arms between Israel and the Arab states and to prevent an arms race in the Middle East. The declaration turned out to be meaningless. Britain refused to sell arms to Israel, although she continued to supply them to Jordan and Iraq. The United States stubbornly insisted on her refusal to provide Israel with arms, although she realized the danger in store from Egypt. Instead, the American State Department agreed to advise Canada and France to sell Israel a small number of jet planes. Canada hesitated for a long time, as, under the circumstances, was quite understandable. The United States continued to refuse to sell arms to Israel although American weapons were sent to Iraq and Saudi Arabia. Britain sold heavy tanks to Nasser but would not sell them to Israel. Certain powers seemed to be competing to be the first to win over the Middle Eastern dictators.

With all the modesty becoming a spokesman of a small nation, but with the moral force of a son of Israel, I felt it my duty to tell the nations of the world that the men and women of Israel would not be led like sheep to the slaughter. In Israel we had gathered together the veteran rebuilders of our Homeland, the remnants of Hitler's victims, Jewish refugees from the Arab countries, and Jews returning to Zion from a free and prosperous dispersion. Not many peoples had battled so fiercely for freedom and survival. We would fight on. What Hitler had done to six

71

million helpless Jews in the ghettos of Europe no enemy of Israel would do to free men rooted in their own soil.

After the War of Independence, we offered our hand in peace to the Arabs who had tried to destroy us, but they rejected it. The Armistice Agreements were not honored, and the Arab states warred against us by boycott and blockade, and by sending marauders across our borders. During the first nine months of 1955, incursions from the Gaza Strip alone cost us 153 dead and wounded. The Suez Canal was barred to us. Egypt was attempting to block the Straits of Tiran to Israeli shipping. This warfare would have to stop; we could not allow it to remain one-sided any longer.

On November 2, 1955, in presenting my new Government to the Knesset, I declared:

> The Government of Israel is prepared, as before, faithfully to observe the Armistice Agreements in every detail, in the letter and the spirit. But this duty applies equally to the other side. An agreement violated by the other side will not be binding on us either. If the Armistice lines are opened to saboteurs and murderers from across the border . . . they shall not be closed again to the defenders and fighters. If our rights are violated by acts of violence on land or at sea, we shall preserve freedom of action to defend our rights in the most effective manner possible.

Our hearts were set on peace, we coveted no inch of foreign soil, but as long as we lived we would permit no man to rob us of a single inch of ours.

To dispel the dangers of the situation, I was prepared to meet Nasser or any other Arab ruler, without prior conditions, at the earliest possible moment. My Government was ready to enter into a peace settlement, with guarantees for long-term political, economic, and cultural co-operation with all our neighbors. If the Arabs were not ready for this, we would accept a limited arrangement: guarantees for the full implementation of the Armistice Agreements; the prevention of offenses by either party; the cessation of all acts of hostility, boycott, and blockade; the observance of freedom of the seas; and other mutually agreeable provisions. We offered the Arabs the chance to show the world what they really wanted: war or peace.

On November 9, 1955, Sir Anthony Eden, then British Prime Minister, delivered a speech at the Guildhall in London on the situation in the Middle East. Sir Anthony condemned the Czechoslovakia-Egypt deal, which was calculated "to inject a new element of danger" into the Middle East and "to deliver weapons of war—tanks, airplanes, even submarines—to one side only." He went on to say that "we find it impossible to reconcile this Soviet action with protestations that they wish to end the 'cold war' in the new spirit of Geneva. . . . It is fantastic to pretend that this deliberate act of policy was an innocent commercial transaction."

He went on to argue that the main responsibility must lie not with the recipients but with the suppliers of the arms. At the same time, although he complained of the Soviet Union's action, he did not give the slightest hint of any intention on Britain's part to change her own policy of supplying arms "to one side only."

He expressed his concern at the growing tension in the Middle East and especially between Egypt and Israel. "The hostility of Israel and her neighbors is unreconciled," he said. "Here time has proved no healer." But he did not find it necessary to add that Israel, which had

73

been the victim of attack in 1948, had harbored no grudge against her neighbors and had offered them her hand in peace.

Then Sir Anthony proceeded to single out Israel as a sacrifice in his proposals for easing the tension. Israel, he said, must cede some of her territory to the Arabs, and this he termed a "compromise." Why did Sir Anthony use that word to describe the truncation of Israel's territory? It was necessary, he said, to find a "compromise" between the two sets of frontiers, and part of the "superfluous" territory of Israel should be handed over to the Arabs.

I felt that his comment on the "innocent commercial transaction" between Czechoslovakia and Egypt applied with a greater measure of force to his own "compromise." His proposal had warrant neither in law, in morals, nor in logic. Far from improving relations and bringing a settlement nearer, it was likely to encourage Arab aggressiveness and diminish the prospects of peace. Sir Anthony had overlooked a succession of basic historical and political facts on which, as the man for many years in charge of the Foreign Office, he could not have been uninformed.

History does not begin with the United Nations resolution of November 29, 1947. The Jewish people will always remember with gratitude that thirty years before that resolution the British Government, under the leadership of Lloyd George and Balfour, and with the active cooperation of President Woodrow Wilson, acknowledged the historical connection between the Jewish people and the Land of Israel. But this connection did not come into existence as a result of the Balfour Declaration: the opposite was the case. It was in existence throughout the generations, and we live in our Land by right and not on sufferance. There was a State of Israel when human history knew nothing of Britain or America, and Jerusalem was its capital long before London, Moscow, or Paris was founded.

The British Government was the only non-Arab government to declare in the Assembly of the United Nations, as early as September 26, 1947, that it would not implement the United Nations Resolution on the Palestine problem; it lived up to its declaration, and so, directly or indirectly, encouraged armed Arab resistance to the resolution. The British Government refused to hand over the administration of Palestine to a United Nations Commission during the transition period and abandoned the country to chaos. Only the establishment of the Government of Israel on May 14, 1948, eight hours before the British withdrew, had saved the Jewish community from destruction and the country from ruin. When Egypt, Syria, Iraq, Lebanon, Trans-Jordan, and Saudi Arabia did not stop at public avowals of disagreement and opposition but sent their armies into Israel as soon as the Mandatory Government left, in an attempt to destroy an ancient State which had been re-established by decree of more than two-thirds of the members of the United Nations, neither Britain nor any other member state made the least move to save us. Worse still, British officers of the Arab Legion and British arms in other Arab hands played a conspicuous part in the attacks on Jerusalem.

What Sir Anthony proposed—to increase the area of the neighboring states (Egypt, Jordan, Syria, and Lebanon) by dismembering Israel itself—had not entered the mind of a single member of the United Nations Assembly. According to the United Nations Resolution not an inch of Palestine territory was to be handed over to

75

the neighboring states. Sir Anthony's proposal, in effect, amounted to rewarding the Arabs for their aggression of 1948.

The only state in the Middle East entitled to redress was the State of Israel. The Arab states still continued their war by blockade, boycott, and the organization of bands of terrorists who crossed our borders to commit murder and sabotage. The presence of the Egyptian army in the Gaza Strip was in contradiction to the United Nations resolution. The annexation by the Jordan Government of a considerable part of western Palestine —the Old City of Jerusalem, Hebron, Nablus, and other areas—was also in contradiction to the resolution. The British Government, and I believe only the British Government, recognized this annexation in April, 1950, completely ignoring the resolution. If Sir Anthony was correct in his contention that "it is not right, I agree, that United Nations resolutions should be ignored," then Egypt should have immediately left the Gaza Strip and Jordan should have evacuated all western Palestine.

Sir Anthony's proposal was not a method for resolving the conflict in the Middle East; instead, it would aggravate it.

My own offer stood—to meet any or all of the Arab rulers without prior conditions. There was room for mutually beneficial frontier adjustments, but Sir Anthony's counsel to slice up our territory put a premium on aggression. The Government of Israel could not conduct negotiations on such a basis.

It is an understatement to say that the events of that autumn of 1955 caused us deep concern. The Czech-Egyptian arms deal had transformed our security situation from one of perhaps reasonable inferiority to one of grave disadvantage. The deal was the clearest possible evidence of a radical switch of Communist policy to full support of the ambitions of the Egyptian dictator and, as a corollary, hostility to Israel. This sharpening of the Communist world's pro-Arab and anti-Israel policies may or may not have been brought about by the assumption that Nasser could be weaned from the West, and the Middle East be turned into one more focus of trouble for the Western powers. In any event, those policies, taking the active form they did, could only be carried through at heavy cost to the State of Israel and grave risk to its security.

In November, 1955, Parliament approved the Government's program, which I had submitted when I resumed the office of Prime Minister. In that program the Government dedicated itself to the following objectives in the spheres of foreign affairs and security:

1. To improve our military preparedness and the organization, equipment, training, and morale of the Israel Defense Forces both in the regular army and in the reserves; to endeavor to integrate the border settlements within the national defense framework;

2. To relax the tense situation along the borders by taking effective measures for the protection of frontier settlements and other vulnerable areas;

3. To work unceasingly for the achievement of peaceful relations with the Arab states;

4. To continue to observe meticulously the Armistice Agreements between Israel and her neighbors; to continue to insist on their equal observance of the agreements;

5. To base our relations with other nations on a sincere aspiration toward the strengthening of peace in the world as a whole, and particularly in the Middle

77

East; on our needs in the spheres of immigration, security, development, and economic and political independence; on the needs of the Jews in the Diaspora; and on a faithful adherence to the principles of the Charter of the United Nations;

6. To foster relations of friendship and mutual assistance with every peace-loving nation irrespective of its domestic regime and without prejudicing the interests of any other nation;

7. To continue our efforts to establish reciprocal relations of friendship with the nations of Asia;

8. To strengthen our ties with all countries where Jews lived and which permitted their Jewish communities to share in the reconstruction of Israel;

9. To seek wider sympathy for the policy of ingathering the exiles and permission for Jewish immigration from all countries;

10. To disassociate ourselves from any aggressive trend or alliance directed against any state whatsoever and to help, insofar as possible, to reduce international tension; and

11. To maintain Israel's full sovereignty, territorial integrity, independence, and democratic regime, and to insure that her relations with other countries are based on equality, reciprocity, and the prevention of aggression.

We were disturbed by rumors of warlike preparations in Syria, in unison with Egypt and Jordan. These three states had just concluded a pact which we had grounds for believing was an aggressive alliance against Israel. Shortly before, we had had occasion to grow suspicious of Syrian activities, and almost simultaneously with the news of the Czechoslovak-Egyptian arms deal we had learned of the movement of Egyptian units into the southern frontier zone, which had been demilitarized under the Armistice Agreement but part of which was regarded as Egyptian territory and part, with the settlement of Nitzana as its center, as Israeli.

The presence of these Egyptian army units in the demilitarized zone, through which ran the main highway from Sinai into Israel, and which was adjacent to the Egyptian-held Gaza Strip, was a direct challenge to the United Nations and, failing action by that body, to Israel. The United Nations did not secure the withdrawal of the Egyptians and, in October, 1955, after the Egyptians had moved into positions around Nitzana itself and Cairo had three times ignored the United Nations demand for withdrawal, we felt we had no alternative but to take action ourselves. In a swift operation, our defense forces ejected the Egyptians and destroyed the bases they had set up in the demilitarized zone.

Like other actions we had been compelled to take that autumn and winter, the Nitzana operation had been forced upon us by the obviously aggressive nature of the Egyptian bases, which had served as training centers for marauders and especially for the *fedayun*, whose raids were carried out after military briefings. The supply of Soviet arms to Egypt and the concentration of the major part of those arms in Sinai gave the murderous raids of the *fedayun* and the bases from which they were launched a new and more threatening significance.

Chapter Five
Tension on the Borders

The Nitzana operation was carried out in October, 1955. Before the end of that year we had recourse to yet another severe operation, this time against the Syrians. Lake Kinneret, known also as Lake Tiberias or the Sea of Galilee, is wholly within Israel territory, as it had always, indeed, been within the territory of Mandatory Palestine. The Syrians, however, are in possession of the high ground rising from the eastern shore of the lake, and for several years had harassed our fishermen with rifle and machine-gun fire from concealed positions on the slope held by Syrian army units. Many fishermen had been killed. The Syrians had been active also against our settlers cultivating the land by the Jordan where it flows into the lake, and had caused many casualties. The situation had worsened and we had every reason to believe that the increased Syrian activity against our fishermen and farmers had been undertaken in co-ordination with the increasing raiding by *fedayun* from the Egyptian bases in the south.

Our action took place on the night of December 11 to 12 and was highly successful. Syrian positions overlooking the lake were destroyed; some artillery and twenty-nine prisoners were taken. Having failed utterly to persuade the United Nations to take effective measures when the Arab states violated the Armistice Agreements they had signed with us under U.N. auspices, we were bound to take punitive (rather than retaliatory) action ourselves as the only means of defending the lives of our citizens. The raid of December 11-12 against the Syrians was the subject of loud criticism internationally. I was convinced, however, that in my capacity as Prime Minister and Minister of Defense I had done the necessary and proper thing—and indeed could not have done less without failing in my responsibilities to the people—in ordering both the Nitzana and Lake Kinneret operations.

Alternatives had proved fruitless. Following deadly raids into our border areas—and the State of Israel, by comparison with other countries, is sheer border area over much of its length and narrow breadth—we were entitled to protest to one or other of the Mixed Armistice Commissions set up by the U.N. to hear such complaints. We had complained over and over again—to no purpose. All a Mixed Armistice Commission could do was to pronounce guilt and censure the guilty. There was no preventive or deterrent action it could take. The Commission would meet, hear the accusations, listen to the counteraccusations, declare guilt, and then adjourn. The following night there would be another raid, with a few more Israeli settlers or fishermen killed, a powerhouse blown up, a road mined. Complaints to the Security Council could not be made over the heads of the Mixed

Armistice Commissions, but even where such a complaint was authorized, duly lodged and heard, and a decision taken, nothing came of the decision. Neither United Nations decisions nor United Nations observers have been able to prevent violations of the Charter and the Armistice Agreements or protect our citizens against incessant attacks across our borders in the south, the east, and the north.

Section Eight of the Armistice Agreement with Jordan provides for the orderly reactivation of the cultural and humanitarian institutions on Mount Scopus and free access to them, free access to the holy places and cultural institutions, and use of the cemetery on the Mount of Olives. I appealed in this matter to the United Nations Secretary-General, the late Dag Hammarskjold. He approached the Jordan Government—which turned a deaf ear to his plea. To this day the Hebrew University and Hadassah Hospital installations on Mount Scopus are standing idle; we are denied free access to the Western ("Wailing") Wall and the other Jewish holy places across the Armistice lines; we are barred from our ancient cemetery on the Mount of Olives.

The Security Council decided twice—in 1951 and 1956—that we are fully entitled to free passage through the Suez Canal, but to this day the Suez remains closed to us and the United Nations does nothing.

We could not sit with folded hands in the face of attempts on the lives of our citizens by marauders sent into our sovereign territory by our neighbors in violation of the Armistice Agreements. In 1951, cutthroats sent into Israel from across the borders killed or wounded 137 of our citizens. In 1952 there were 147 casualties; in 1953 the figure rose to 162, and in 1954 to 180. In 1955 *fedayun* activity from Egypt increased, and 258 Israelis were killed or injured. The Egyptians also became experts at mining Israel's transport arteries, and in 1955 alone 49 persons were killed by mines.

This guerilla war did not draw enough world attention for one simple reason: the killings and minings were not carried out on a mass scale or in one big operation; and the scattered killing of two or three Israelis a week was not considered sensational news by the world press and was not featured prominently in the daily headlines.

Egypt's representatives at the United Nations—Mahmoud Fawzi on June 16, 1951, Abdul Hamid Ghaleb on February 16, 1954, and Mahmoud Azmi on March 13, 1954—expressly declared that Egypt considered that a state of war continued to exist between her and Israel, despite the fact that the Security Council had stated in no uncertain terms that a state of war could not be reconciled with the Armistice Agreement.

From the events which led to the Peloponnesian War onward into our own times, Governments have felt compelled to react to this kind of provocation much as the Israeli Government did. The United States Government sent troops into Mexico on March 15, 1916, after having failed to put an end by peaceful means to Mexican marauding in the frontier zones. The American forces were not withdrawn until early in 1917. In a note to the Mexican Government, the Secretary of State of the day, Robert Lansing, referred to conditions of violence which had thrown the frontier of the United States "into a constant state of apprehension and turmoil." Representations had been made to the Mexican Government, and the U.S. Government had waited "month after month for the consummation of its hope and expectation." The note complained that the Mexican Government had been "unable, or possibly considered it inadvisable, to apprehend and punish" the marauders. It emphasized the fact that no Government whose territory was subject to such raids could be expected to maintain along its frontier a force of such strength as to be able to prevent the incursions. The note goes on to state:

> The most effective method of preventing raids of this nature, as past experience has fully demonstrated, is to visit punishment or destruction on the raiders. . . . The first duty of any Government is the protection of life and property. This is the paramount obligation for which governments are instituted, and governments neglecting or failing to perform it are not worthy of the name.

Such arguments, however, coming from Israel, made little impression. I determined, nevertheless, to make a further appeal to the Chief of Staff of the United Nations Truce Supervisory Organization, General Burns, to use his authority and undoubted skill in an attempt to bring about stable conditions along the frontiers and to secure, above all, the co-operation of the Egyptian Government, whose aggressive policy had begun to influence our other neighbors.

On December 5, 1955, I met General Burns, giving him the text of the Government's program (see page 77) and asking him to find out from the Egyptian authorities whether or not they were ready to order an immediate cease-fire; to observe the Armistice Agreement in full, including all its articles, as we undertook to do; and to accept proposals for the observance of the Armistice Agreement which had been submitted to them and to us on November 2 by the Secretary-General of the United Nations, Dag Hammarskjold.

General Burns went to Egypt and on December 11 came to see me again. A very punctilious person, he did not say that the Egyptians rejected the cease-fire proposal, refused to comply with the Armistice Agreement, and objected to Mr. Hammarskjold's proposals, but he admitted that they did not undertake to carry out a cease-fire (in fact, they had been firing at our patrols and border settlements almost every day), did not promise to comply with the Armistice Agreement, and did not agree to the Secretary-General's proposals. I found it difficult to grasp the subtle difference in practice between rejection of a proposal and failure to accept it.

The tension on the borders continued, and the failure of General Burns's mission left us no choice. We were compelled to adopt deterrent measures to protect the lives of our citizens and to safeguard the country's borders. Whenever raids into our territory became serious, the Government first appealed to the United Nations Observers to make an effort to correct the situation. When, as was customary, the Observers did not succeed, the Israeli security forces would then be brought into operation against the base of the aggression. The forces carrying out such punitive operations were thoroughly disciplined and never went beyond their orders, which included the injunction to avoid harming civilians. Our policy was plain and I had stated it again and again. If the Armistice lines were to be open to saboteurs and murderers, they could not be closed to the defenders. If our rights and our people's lives were assailed by acts of violence, we reserved freedom of action to take such measures as we thought fit to safeguard those rights and lives. That policy we had applied at Nitzana, and, after General Burns had returned empty-handed from Cairo, we were compelled to apply it again at Lake Kinneret.

Such punitive actions were almost invariably followed by periods of relative tranquillity in the area which had been subject to the action. However, as the raids extended along our frontiers, increasing in severity and revealing an organization of clearly military origin, and with bases in Jordan and Syria supplementing those in Egypt, the strain upon our people and indeed upon our resources became intolerable.

Week in, week out, we demanded effective steps by the United Nations representatives to put an end to these murderous attacks, but in vain. They showed themselves impotent to insure peace on the borders. I do not accuse these emissaries of the United Nations of lack of good will; they simply had no way to compel our neighbors to keep their promises.

Our right to self-defense was not only a natural right; it was expressly stated in the Charter in Article 51. Some of the United Nations personnel denied us this right. They stigmatized as "reprisals" the defensive measures we took against the murders organized by Egypt and Jordan. All the United Nations Observers and representatives knew as well as we that the *fedayun* worked under orders from the Arab Governments, with Egypt taking the central position. Captured *fedayun* had admitted these things in our courts, and the Egyptian Minister of Religious Endowments, Hassan al-Bakuri, said the same thing in a broadcast from a Cairo radio station under Nasser's control: "There is no reason why the *fedayun*, who hate their enemies, should not penetrate deep into Israel, and make the lives of her people a hell."

We, however, refused to allow Israel to be turned into a hell. Those who stigmatized our actions as "reprisals" and denied us the right of self-defense guaranteed by the Charter were simply giving the green light to those re-

86

sponsible for the *fedayun,* allowing the marauders to continue to strike with impunity. Egypt and Jordan would have to learn that those who caused the deaths of so many Israelis, of all walks of life, would not escape the consequences.

To my regret, for some time the United Nations authorities had shown an inclination to transform the Armistice Agreements into a one-sided obligation on our part toward the United Nations, absolving the other signatories, for all practical purposes, from their commitments toward us. They shut their eyes to such transgressions as Jordan's persistent disregard of Article VIII, which promised free access to the Wailing Wall and our other holy places. In no other chapter of Jerusalem's history since the Second Temple fell, whether under Byzantine tyranny, Arab conquest, Seljuks and Crusaders, Turks, or Mandatory Britain, had Jews been debarred from worship at that sacred relic of the Temple.

Against Jordan's recalcitrance, the United Nations staff did nothing. It was the same deplorable story when it came to a resumption of activity in the Hebrew University, the National Library and the Hadassah Hospital on Mount Scopus, access to the Jewish cemetery on the Mount of Olives, and the use of the Latrun-Jerusalem highway. Our pleas of religious and national attachment, of cultural values, went unheeded. We saw no sign of activity on the part of the United Nations authorities to right these wrongs.

Not to be outdone, Egypt brushed aside the Armistice ban on the deployment of armed forces on the Kuseima-Abu Ageila line, near the Gaza Strip, and would not permit United Nations Observers near the area.

We could not submit to the silent condonation of these

87

and many similar violations of the Armistice Agreements, or the disposition of United Nations personnel to regard Israel as an international zone, in complete disregard of Article 2 of the Charter, which declares that the United Nations Organization is based on the principle of the sovereign equality of all its members.

The Security Council's incapacity to implement its 1951 decision on freedom of navigation in the Suez Canal made no small contribution to the impotence of the United Nations personnel in Israel. All the same, this personnel, which exposed every difference between itself and us on matters outside its jurisdiction, never once reported to the Council that the Arab Governments had all along been violating the principles and provisions of the Charter.

The first paragraph of the Charter defines the object of the United Nations as the safeguarding of international peace and security and provides that collective measures must be taken for the prevention and removal of threats to peace. The Arab press and radio were full of such threats; so were the public speeches of Nasser, the King of Jordan, the Syrian President, and King Saud. Nothing had been done by the United Nations personnel in those countries for "the prevention and removal" of these threats.

Paragraph 1 of the United Nations Charter also requires adjustment or settlement of international disputes by peaceful means. Year after year we had asked for that, had offered to meet the Arab leaders, if only to stop aggression; our voice had been like the voice of one that crieth in the wilderness. We had also protested, in vain, that the Arab states were conducting an economic boycott and blockade against us in defiance of Article 2 of the Charter. What had the United Nations authorities done, or attempted to do, to safeguard our elementary rights, to prevent, and bring to an end, these acts of hostility against us? Such was the situation at the end of 1955 and so it continued into 1956. In addition to what might be called external crises, and the frustrating search for armaments to match those going into Egypt and piling up in the Sinai Peninsula, we had, of course, our internal problems—and our internal successes.

Just as I was convinced that, in the absence of other effective means, there was no alternative to using the security forces against the bases of raiding gangs operating from Egypt, Jordan, or Syria, so was I convinced that war was not inevitable. Early in January, 1956, I expressed this view to the assembled Knesset in the name of every member of the Cabinet, and added that we should call upon the nation to undertake a voluntary and concerted effort to strengthen our defenses, heighten the morale of the border settlements, and consolidate our economy, in order to avoid war.

In the ensuing discussion some members of the Knesset disagreed with me, arguing that we were already in a state of war and that we should institute an emergency regime. I welcomed the differing opinions because I felt that in a matter so grave as the one which confronted us it was every man's duty to say what was in his heart. I considered, however, that these views were not only mistaken but harmful.

Any dispassionate observer would indeed admit that we were living in times as critical as 1947. It was impossible to call the situation we had endured for more than seven years a state of peace. However, there is a difference between war and lack of peace.

War can determine a people's destiny: freedom or bondage, survival or death. Though it may be permissible to use figurative phrasing and hyperbole in the realm of poetry and imagery, we must be meticulously precise in our choice of words when discussing this momentous issue. Those who suggested that we were already at war, therefore, were either committing a most reprehensible error of speech or were incapable of distinguishing between war and the lack of peace.

It was true that no treaty of peace had been concluded. There were only Armistice Agreements, and even these were violated more often than not by our neighbors, who trespassed on our territory and dispatched their guerillas to strike at our citizens and their property.

A danger of war existed, a danger neither fictional nor far away, but war was not certain. It could be avoided. If we could get arms not inferior in quality to those the Communists were supplying to Egypt, we could be almost sure that Nasser would not dare to attack us.

Lack of peace is not a desirable situation either, and sooner or later one may slide into war, but frontier skirmishes are not war. Against the skirmishes and infractions of the last seven years we had by no means been helpless; we were well able to defend ourselves and hit back. Skirmishes had been our lot long before the State arose, yet at no time did we halt the immigration and constructive endeavour to which ultimately we owed our statehood.

Under the unstable Armistice regime we had persevered and intensified our efforts in every direction, so that in seven years we had accomplished more than in the preceding seventy, and created the best military force in the Middle East. All of this had been accomplished in a period of lack of peace. I pointed out these achievements to my critics; it was not the first time in our

90

history that we had had to work with one hand, while the other grasped the weapon.

However, there had been two cardinal changes since the War of Independence. In 1948, the sympathies of much of the world were with us. Of the arms we fought with, some had been acquired in an Eastern country and others in a Western. The only unfriendly Government had been the British; but the British are a democratic people not bound by Government fiat, so that even there we enjoyed a great deal of good will. Now the situation had altered. The Secretary of the Communist party in the Soviet Union, whose word no Soviet citizen dare contradict, had declared that ever since its establishment as a State, Israel had been hostile to the Arab peoples and a menace to them. Whatever he said, even if irreconcilable with historic truth, was binding on the People's Republics.

The second cardinal change represented a striking transformation at home. From 650,000 souls in 1948, we had grown to almost two and a half times that number. This was an undeniable advantage, but it also meant added responsibilities. Above all, it meant that we were not the uniform, closely knit community we had been in 1948; only potentially, not actually, were we one nation with a more or less common background. The process of integrating the new immigrants was going steadily ahead and had recently been accelerated with the introduction of speedier methods of providing permanent and comfortable homes for the newcomers in development areas. At the same time, we had considerably increased agricultural and industrial output, and, driven by the Arab boycott and the fact that our natural market, the Middle East, was denied to us, we had succeeded

91

in opening up valuable export markets beyond the seas. We had even tapped a source of oil at Heletz, near Ashkelon, which, although it provided only a small part of our local needs, had reduced the strain and cost of importing oil from Venezuela—more convenient markets were closed to us because of the Suez Canal blockade—and had encouraged us to hope for richer deposits.

One way and another, therefore, we were trying to establish sound economic foundations upon which to build. The fact remains, however, that we had lagged behind in the process of effectively settling and integrating the new immigrants and certainly were in no condition to wage war if we could possibly help it.

On the eve of Independence Day, 1956 (which fell that year on May 15), I reviewed what we had accomplished and what yet lay before us.

In the ninth year of our independence, our enemies were scheming against us, saying, as in days of old: " 'Come, and let us cut them off from being a nation; that the name of Israel may be no more in remembrance' " (Psalms 83:5). There was neither despair nor fear in us when we faced our adversaries then; there would be none if we must face them again. We would not be thrown into panic by the *fedayun* in ambush or vanquished by the hordes of Amalek* who gathered now beyond our borders. And we would not be misled by political intrigues of specious lovers of peace. Our trust was in the Rock of Israel, and with that trust we would meet all visible or veiled designs to jeopardize our independence, our territory, or our peace.

Defense had now become our chief preoccupation, but we would not for a moment interrupt the creative work

* The Amalekites were the first to attack the Children of Israel after the Exodus from Egypt.

which was Israel's ultimate goal. Unlike other states, ours was born of a great and glorious vision of the prophets of redemption for Israel and all mankind, proclaimed from the hills of Jerusalem and living on in Jewish hearts for thousands of years.

In the proclamation that set up our State anew, we had enunciated the ideals for the sake of which we had established it: the ingathering of the exiles, the flowering of the wastelands, and the creation of a regime of justice and peace. This is what we had then promised and would forever perform:

> The State of Israel will be open to Jewish immigration and the ingathering of the exiles. It will devote itself to developing the land for the good of all its inhabitants. It will rest upon foundations of liberty, justice, and peace, as envisioned by the Prophets of Israel.

We had transported about 800,000 immigrants to Israel from every point of the compass. After a brief standstill, the stream of immigration had flowed again; in the year preceding April, 1956, 41,000 Jews had come in.

Throughout the length and breadth of the land, we had established hundreds of new villages, more than in all the previous generations. In the last year, we had established a new region of Lachish in the south on our eastern border, and almost 9,000 newcomers had been sent directly to settlements in that area. We had also built new villages in Galilee, in the Jerusalem Corridor, and on our eastern and western borders.

In the south, we had started a great irrigation scheme to bring the waters of the Yarkon River down to the parched expanses of the Negev and alter the landscape of

Israel. Our first oil well had been drilled in South Judea, and a search for oil started in other areas. The railway had reached Beersheba, city of the Patriarchs and capital of the Negev. A new town, Dimona, was springing up in the Judean Desert, close to the phosphate deposits and the industry centered near the Dead Sea.

With manpower and water flowing southward, the first factories were rising in Kiryat Gat in the heart of the Lachish region. Ashkelon, Beersheba, and Eilat were expanding in area and population, though not as quickly as we wanted.

Our maritime trade was also growing. The commercial fleet was larger, and new, modern ships had been acquired with German reparations funds to buttress our economy and improve our defenses at sea.

We were extending our educational system and encouraging the creation of literature and art and the pursuit of learning, so that Israel was becoming an important, though modest, center of science and research. We wanted to perpetuate the spiritual heritage of our past and to enhance it with the spiritual achievements of our own generation and the generations to come. Once again the light would blaze from Zion to Jews everywhere and to the peoples of all lands. We would integrate the treasures of our tradition with the works of the spirit of the whole human race.

Universal compulsory education in the elementary schools and the cultural program of the Israel Defense Forces were breaking down among the younger generation the barriers between the variegated communities of which our population was composed. These communities, which had come to us from exile, were steadily finding more communication with each other. In 1951 four-fifths of our soldiers corresponded in foreign languages; five years later, just as many wrote their letters in Hebrew. That was one of the remarkable proofs of the cultural absorption of the new immigrants.

Our eighth year of independence had been one of rigorous testing for the Defense Forces. Our enemies in the south and in the east had attacked incessantly. Our units had driven them back, striking hard, but there was no room for complacency or arrogance. We had to press on to enlarge our defensive capacity in every sphere while, at the same time, sparing no effort to maintain peace.

However, the situation on our borders had steadily worsened. Throughout the whole world—except, apparently, in the Arab states—there was deep concern and fear that a conflagration in the Middle East might well extend to envelop the rest of the world. In view of the increased tension, the Secretary-General of the United Nations, Dag Hammarskjold, who had already dashed out from New York to Cairo and Jerusalem in January of 1956, came again in April.

Chapter Six
At Bay

The Secretary-General's mission was clear evidence of the serious situation in the Middle East.

During the early months of 1956, incursions and gunfire from the Gaza Strip went on as before. In February and March our losses were seven killed and thirty-one wounded. In April the situation further deteriorated. Egyptian forces began to cross the border and to shell our settlements along the Gaza Strip: Kissufim, Ein Hashlosha, Nahal Oz, and Nirim.

The activities of the *fedayun* also increased, and hundreds of them penetrated into Israeli territory. In the first twenty days of April alone, we suffered eighty-two casualties among our soldiers and civilians, eighteen killed and sixty-four wounded, including the loathsome murder of children in the synagogue at Shafrir. Eleven *fedayun* were killed and five taken prisoner by our army inside Israel. A wounded Egyptian pilot, whose plane was brought down by our air force in the neighborhood of Sdeh Boker, was also captured.

This intensification of guerilla warfare shed a revealing light on the second, and greater, danger of an all-out Arab attack against Israel. Egypt, after the Czech deal, was fortified with Communist arms, not to mention previous British consignments. Saudi Arabia and Iraq had obtained arms from the United States. The Egyptian, Syrian, and Saudian dictators publicly proclaimed their intention to liquidate Israel.

Public opinion in France, Britain, America, and other Western countries awakened to the imminent danger of war in the Middle East, and their Governments, notably in France, began to be on the alert.

There was, of course, the tripartite declaration of 1950. Its aim was to maintain an equilibrium of forces and arms between Israel and the Arabs as well as to safeguard the integrity of the borders and regional peace. We had not, however, entertained the illusion that this declaration would serve as a barrier to the belligerent designs of the Arab rulers. In the War of Independence and thereafter, we had learned the hard lesson: only if we ourselves had strength would we have peace. If we lacked strength, no one would take our part.

The Czech deal, and the subsequent unwillingness of America and Britain to rectify the imbalance by selling us defensive arms, made the declaration meaningless, and war drew nearer with every jet plane and heavy bomber that reached Egypt. It was true that others besides ourselves had at least realized that the one thing that might deter the Arab alliance from pouncing on Israel was a counterbalancing supply of defensive arms to us. The Government of France, the first to act, sold us twenty-four Mystère jets. We were most grateful for this

97

response, but substantial though it was, it was still far from meeting the barest minimum of our total needs.

On April 9 the following statement was issued by the White House:

> The President and the Secretary of State regard the situation (in the Middle East) with the utmost seriousness. . . .
>
> The United States, in accordance with its responsibilities under the Charter of the United Nations, will observe its commitments with constitutional means to oppose any aggression in the area.
>
> The United States is likewise determined to support and assist any nation which might be subjected to such aggression.

We were advised to rely on the U.N. Charter, but we could hardly accept the Charter alone as a sufficient guarantee of Israel's security or as a deterrent to the aggressive plans of our neighbors. The Charter had been there in 1948 when the Arab states invaded us but had moved no member state to come to our rescue. We did not minimize the importance of a promise from the White House to come to the assistance of any nation suffering aggression in the Middle East, for Israel was the only state in the Middle East likely to suffer that fate, but if American help was not given in time, the good will of the statement was likely to show itself as too late and too feeble.

What we expected of America was not the dispatch of troops against an aggressor after his attack had begun; we wanted the dispatch of defensive arms to Israel to deter and forestall aggression. We believed that external military intervention in the Middle East would precipitate a grave threat to world peace, and that war could be prevented only by achieving a balance of arms between Israel and her Arab neighbors. The longer defensive arms were withheld from us, the greater and closer the risk of war.

This was the atmosphere in which Dag Hammarskold's April visit took place. He had come to look into the various aspects of the working of the Armistice Agreements, especially the one between Egypt and Israel, and, in consultation with all parties, to contrive arrangements for reducing friction on the borders.

On two points there was a complete identity of views between him and ourselves: (1) that all parties must honor and obey all the clauses of the agreements in letter and spirit; and (2) that Article II, paragraph 2, in the agreement between Israel and Egypt should be singled out and its observance made paramount and obligatory, even if the remaining clauses were not fulfilled.

I have already referred to this paragraph, but I want to reproduce it here in the specific context of the agreement between Egypt and Israel:

> No element of the land, sea, or air military or para-military forces of either Party, including non-regular forces, shall commit any warlike or hostile act against the military or para-military forces of the other Party, or against civilians in territory under the control of that Party; or shall advance beyond or pass over for any purpose whatsoever the Armistice Demarcation Line set forth in Article VI of this Agreement; and elsewhere shall not violate the international frontier.

We assured the Secretary-General at the beginning of our conversations that the Government of Israel had always been and was still prepared to observe each agreement in its entirety and in every detail on a basis of reciprocity. The Government of Israel was also prepared in particular, even in divorce from the other clauses, to undertake to observe faithfully Article II, paragraph 2, again provided the other side did the same.

On April 17, the day of Hammarskjold's arrival in Jerusalem, I had signed a letter to him, on behalf of the Government, which reads as follows:

> I write to confirm, on behalf of the Government of Israel, that, in accordance with Article II (2) of the Egypt-Israel General Armistice Agreement, orders are in force, and have been repeated, for strict observance as from 6:00 P.M. Israel time tomorrow, April 18, 1956, prohibiting any firing by units of the Defence Army of Israel across the Demarcation Line, as well as the crossing of the Demarcation Line by military or para-military forces, including non-regular forces, for any purpose whatsoever. This assurance is given on the understanding of full reciprocity on the part of Egypt.

Mr. Hammarskjold informed us on April 19 that he had a similar undertaking from the Egyptian Government. Our orders went into effect, and we left no room for doubt in his mind that, given reciprocity, the Government of Israel would continue to carry out the other clauses of the agreement in full, and that it set particular store by Article I, which proclaimed four cardinal principles. In essence, Article I stated that (1) resort to military force in the settlement of the Palestine problem was categorically forbidden; (2) neither party might plan or

perpetrate any aggressive action by its armed forces—
land, sea, or air—against the people or the armed forces
of the other; (3) each party was guaranteed the right to
its security and freedom from fear of attack by the armed
forces of the other; and (4) the conclusion of an Armistice Agreement between the two parties was a step toward the restoration of peace.

I must emphasize that Article I was not content with
prohibiting the threat, planning, or undertaking of aggressive actions by one party against the other. It also
bound each party to observe and honor the right of the
other *to security and freedom from fear of attack.* This
third principle was laid down as a special, independent
provision of the agreement.

No one could say how long the Egyptian Government
would loyally keep the pledge, so often broken, which it
had now renewed. Even in the most favorable circumstances, however, the cease-fire did not weaken the
threat presented by the continuous preparations for war
against Israel in which Egypt and its allies were fever-
ishly engaged. There was no sign of Egypt's accepting
the Security Council's ruling that the Armistice Agreement was incompatible with belligerency. Egypt still
maintained a blockade and siege against us in the Suez
Canal and the straits of the Red Sea. We had no grounds
to assume that Egypt was ready to bow to the requirements of the vital first article of the agreement, or to
cease her bitter propaganda, her menacing and warlike
actions, and her maritime interferences. In such circumstances, the danger of war remained and was growing steadily more grave.

My parting words to Dag Hammarskjold were that
if in any neighboring country he found a sincere inclina-

tion toward peace, he could be certain that we on our side would willingly and unconditionally examine every proposal calculated to bring it about.

I had, however, insisted on our right to self-defense. After all, that right is asserted in the United Nations Charter, Article 51 of which states:

> Nothing in the present Charter shall impair the inherent right of individual or collective self-defense if an armed attack occurs against a Member of the United Nations, until the Security Council has taken measures necessary to maintain international peace and security.

Unfortunately, these principles were not universally accepted where Israel was concerned.

The Secretary-General's report on his visit to Israel expressly denied our right to defend ourselves, although, in a thorough discussion of the subject, he was not able to destroy our case. The Arabs had hoped to crush us by force; when they failed, they tried to undermine our economy by means of a boycott and blockade. Not content with these measures, they organized bands of *fedayun* to destroy our internal security. We did not intend to allow them to complete their work and escape the penalty too.

The Secretary-General was to be congratulated on his success in extracting from all our neighbors a renewed undertaking of absolute and unconditional cease-fire and the prohibition of border violations, though one might doubt whether they would keep it for long. We made it clear to him that on no account would we allow our country and its population to remain defenseless against their terror.

In the United Nations, the Soviet Union and Great Britain had drafted a joint declaration on the relations between Israel and the Arab states which referred to "the need to create conditions in which a peaceful settlement on a mutually acceptable basis of the dispute between the parties can be made." But as a result of pressure from the Syrian representative and his Arab colleagues, this passage was withdrawn from the resolution submitted to the Security Council by the British Government. The emasculated version of the resolution was passed on June 4, 1956.

This surrender to Arab pressure was a severe blow to the moral standing of the Security Council as an impartial international authority. As citizens of the world and as free men in our own country, we regretted it, for we wanted the jurisdiction of the United Nations to be universally respected and trusted.

Both Egypt and Jordan were characteristically prompt in breaking their word to Dag Hammarskjold. The Secretary-General had hardly gone when the Egyptians sent *fedayun* to wreck military installations and public buildings in Israel. Raiders, trained by Egyptians, came over from Jordan to sabotage, ambush, and murder. In a speech to mark the British evacuation of the Suez Canal Zone on June 13 Abdel Nasser said: "We must be strong so as with a strong hand to take back the rights of the Palestinian people." On June 11 Abdul Hakim Amer, Egyptian Minister of Defense and recently appointed Supreme Commander of the armies of Egypt, Syria, and Saudi Arabia, declared in Alexandria: "The danger of Israel no longer exists. The Egyptian army is sufficiently strong to wipe Israel off the face of the earth." On June 28 Sabri el Assali, Prime Minister of Syria, stated in the Damascus Parliament: "Our foreign policy is based on

103

war against imperialist Zionism and Israel, non-recognition of the theft of Palestine, opposition to peace with Israel, and intensification of the blockade against her."

On July 26, 1956, Egypt announced the nationalization of the Suez Canal.

Chapter Seven
The Ring Tightens

Egypt's unilateral decision to nationalize the Suez Canal brought her into conflict with Britain and France, as the main holders of shares in the company responsible for its construction and operation. There was dismay among the majority of maritime nations, not only because they distrusted Egypt's assurances that the Canal would continue to be efficiently operated, and its profits used for essential improvements, but also because of the evidence of what looked like increasing Communist influence in Cairo.

For our part, we were not in principle opposed to the nationalization of the Suez Canal. However, the occasion was ominous, and the decision represented a new and alarming stage in the development of Nasser's arrogant self-confidence, which had been fortified in proportion to his build-up of Communist arms. For the world at large, the nationalization of the Suez Canal was seen not merely as a blow directed at Britain and France but also as a move in the Cold War. From 1945 to 1950, the Cold War had been concentrated in Europe. For the five years thereafter, from the outbreak of hostilities in Korea until after the end of the fighting in Indo-China, it had been shifted to the Far East. Now, however, it was centered on the Middle East, and no one could foresee the outcome.

Immediately following Nasser's decision to take the Suez Canal to himself, the British Government, which had been the principal shareholder in the Canal Company, called a conference in London to be attended by the various countries whose vital interests had been affected by the Egyptian action. For reasons of its own, the British Government failed to invite Israel to the London conference, although Israel had been the one country consistently injured by Egypt's arbitrary blockading of the Canal. When the Soviet Union submitted to the British Government a long list of countries other than those already invited, and claimed their right to attend, the list included, among other singular "Canal users," the Hashemite Kingdom of Jordan; but again, the State of Israel was overlooked.

We approached the genuine Canal users and some other countries with the request that in their deliberations at the London conference they should secure for Israel the same right of navigation in the Suez Canal as was to be enjoyed by other maritime nations. Promises to that effect were given us. The President of the United States, questioned at the time by a journalist on the subject of the blockade of Israeli ships wishing to pass through the Canal, replied that it was an old stigma and most unjust, and in his opinion not in keeping with the Constantinople Treaty. The day before that, the American Secretary of State, Mr. John Foster Dulles, said that Israel, whether belonging to the Canal Users' Association created at the London conference or not, would enjoy all facilities for her ships and cargoes as if she were.

On October 13, 1956, an Anglo-French resolution designed to bring Egypt, Britain, and France together to negotiate a settlement on the operation of the Canal was presented to the Security Council. The first part of the resolution, adopted unanimously, set forth the six basic requirements for settlement of the Canal dispute. These stated that

1. There should be free and open transit through the Canal without discrimination, overt or covert—this covered both political and technical aspects.

2. The sovereignty of Egypt should be respected.

3. The operation of the Canal should be insulated from the politics of any country.

4. The manner of fixing tolls and charges should be decided by agreement between Egypt and the users.

5. A fair proportion of the dues should be allotted to development.

6. In case of disputes, unresolved affairs between the Suez Canal Company and the Egyptian Government should be settled by arbitration, with suitable terms of reference and suitable provisions for the payment of sums found to be due.

The second part of the resolution, outlining steps for negotiations, was vetoed by the Soviet Union.

The fact remained that the resolution of the Security Council again confirmed freedom of passage in the Suez Canal without discrimination, open or covert; and that the Egyptian dictator followed this up, as he had done in similar instances, with the announcement that no Israeli ship would be allowed to pass. Nor did he feel in any way hindered from adopting a similar attitude at the Red Sea entrance to the Gulf of Aqaba and Israel's port of Eilat, at the head of that gulf. In many ways, Nasser's attempted blockade of the Gulf of Aqaba to Israeli shipping was more damaging to us than his blockade of the Suez Canal. For Israel's future economy, and her ties with the Asian and African peoples, freedom of navigation through the Red Sea and the Straits of Tiran, which give on to the Gulf of Aqaba, is vital. The port of Eilat loses almost all its economic value unless shipping through the Red Sea and the Straits is safeguarded in practice. The Egyptian force stationed opposite the island of Yotvat, now known as Tiran, had been equipped with heavy artillery and was capable of shelling any ship attempting to make its way through the narrow passage.

The Security Council resolution reaffirming the freedom of passage through the Suez Canal for ships of all nations without distinction was approved on October 13, 1956. Between July 26, the date of Nasser's announcement of the nationalization of the Canal, and October 13, the date of the Security Council resolution, there had been some relaxation of tension along our border with Egypt. The very day following the end of the Security Council session at which Suez had been debated, *fedayun* attacks were resumed in full force. On that date, October 14, one group of *fedayun*, working to instructions received at a military base in Sinai, was captured in the neighborhood of Sdeh Boker, the pioneering settlement in the Negev where I had spent the year 1954. This was followed day by day with intensified guerilla raids from Jordan, as well as from Egyptian bases in Sinai and the Gaza Strip.

On October 15, the day following the fresh outbreak of border forays, I rose in my place at the Knesset and, as

108

Prime Minister and Minister of Defense, gave members a survey of the situation as I saw it.

I have told of Dag Hammarskjold's efforts, in April, to obtain a cease-fire on Israel's borders and how, after we agreed to observe this section of the Armistice Agreement even though other sections were not being observed by our neighbors, Hammarskjold got similar undertakings from Egypt, Jordan, and Syria. Egypt sent *fedayun* to sabotage military installations and blow up public buildings in Israel, and Egyptian saboteurs again started mining Israel's roads in the south and the Negev. When the Suez crisis broke, the Egyptian border became temporarily quiet and all the killing and sabotage now came from the Jordanian border. But the very next day after the Security Council wound up its discussion of the Suez affair, Egyptian terrorists went into action again, and only yesterday an Egyptian *fedayun* band, sent out by Egyptian officers from Sinai, was captured near Sdeh Boker. Shortly after the Secretary-General left, Jordanians blew up a two-story house in Ezuz, and that same day a police vehicle was attacked near Kfar Saba. Near Kubeiba a tractorist was shot and killed from ambush; a resident of Jerusalem was killed in the south of the city; two Israelis were killed and one wounded by gunfire near Nir Eliyahu. An Israeli policeman was wounded when the vehicle in which he was riding struck a mine near Afula. Near Ein Hatzeva in the Arava a civilian vehicle was attacked and two of the passengers were killed. At Mevasseret Yerushalayim, near the Capital, hand grenades were thrown and two Jewish workers were shot. At Maaleh Hahamisha a grenade was thrown into the children's house. A bus to

109

Eilat was attacked and four Israelis were killed and nine wounded. In the Duweina area, six Israeli soldiers were killed and two wounded. At Ein Ofarim, three Israeli Druze watchmen were killed.

For weeks following the renewal of the Egyptian and Jordanian attacks we kept pressing United Nations representatives to take practical steps to get the Arab states to desist. But all our pleas and demands were in vain. I do not accuse the United Nations representatives of ill will. But they clearly demonstrated their inability to force our neighbors to fulfill their promises and undertakings.

I summed up my review of our security situation as follows:

It is our desire and our right to live, work and produce in our Homeland in tranquillity and security, for our aim is peace; but we must not close our eyes to the disturbing developments in the area. We must stand guard with open eyes, with good will and foresight, with determination and increased military capacity. *We are compelled to make a supreme effort for security.* It is forced upon us by external factors and hostile forces. *We are perhaps facing momentous decisions and events.* Let us stand ready and united, and the Rock of Israel will not fail.

In fact, our defensive situation had much improved over the previous two or three months. Arms are not the kind of merchandise you can go into a shop, pick out, and take home, provided you have the cash or credit. Throughout the year we had been knocking at many a

110

door but had found most doors barred against us. Britain, after consistently refusing us any arms, although supplying heavy tanks to Nasser, which obviously were intended for use against Israel, had sold us some Meteors. Several types of defensive weapons had reached us from other sources. The United States, while recognizing in principle the need to rectify the arms balance in the Middle East, continued to refuse to supply us with defensive arms but encouraged some of her allies to help us. In this way, Canada had agreed to sell us twenty-four Sabre Jets. With such help as I have indicated, we would have been in a poor way, however, if it had not been for France.

In the survey of events and prospects I gave before the Knesset on October 15, I was able to tell of the generous and invaluable response to our appeal given by the French Government when M. Guy Mollet, the French Socialist leader, was Prime Minister and M. Bourgès-Maunoury, of the Radical party, was his Minister of Defense. The way had thus been opened for the acquisition of modern arms of superior quality, including jet-propelled warplanes, tanks, artillery, and certain modern devices of remarkable efficacy.

These weapons greatly improved the Israel Defense Forces' capacity to resist, but Egypt still had a tremendous superiority in armament. She had destroyers and submarines, which Israel did not possess, and her heavy tanks—British, Czech, and Soviet—jet planes, and bombers were superior in quantity and quality to anything we had, even after the receipt of the arms from France. But for all that, we were not so defenseless as we had been at the beginning of the year. To a group of new officers, our Chief of Staff, General Dayan, was able to say these words:

111

You will be officers in a strong army. The Israel army is strong not because it has armaments which are superior to those of its enemies. It is strong just because its fighting is not dependent on the possession of superior arms. The State is strong, not because it has allies who will hasten to its help if it should be attacked, but because even without allies it will fight to the finish. The Israel army is strong because its sailors, airmen, and soldiers are young men and women whose devotion to the security of their country knows no bound or limit.

Of course, effective, adequate, and modern weapons were of vital importance, and they could be secured only from those friendly nations who sincerely wished to safeguard the peace of the entire area. We once again pressed our demand for adequate defensive arms on the United States, which did not want war in the Middle East and wished both Israel and the Arab peoples well. The Arab rulers, intoxicated by the abundant supplies of arms at their disposal, never ceased to agitate in their public pronouncements for a war to the death with Israel. The value of human life was of secondary importance for them.

Those nations, then, that continued to send arms for aggressive purposes to the Arabs and at the same time denied defensive arms to Israel would have to shoulder the responsibility for the peace of the Middle East and of the world. Almost every day, the statements of Communist leaders repeated their longings for peace. I did not want to doubt the sincerity of these statements, but the Egyptian soldiers, who were being trained to handle the tanks, planes, guns, submarines, and destroyers sent by the Communist countries, received instructions and declarations from their own commanders which were quite incompatible with these utterances.

The situation in the Middle East was further complicated by rivalries among the Arab powers themselves. We had always been aware that Nasser had far-reaching ambitions to impose his rule on all the Arab countries and that the first victim, according to his plan, would be Jordan. In the good old days of normal relations between Britain and Egypt, Nasser believed that he might succeed in annexing—with Britain's assistance or consent— a part of our Negev for the purpose of building a land bridge between Egypt and Jordan. When external forces inimical to Britain gave their support to Nasser's imperialistic aims in the Middle East, a rival Anglo-Iraqi plan took shape. This plan was to annex Jordan to Iraq, and the initial step would be to send Iraqi armed forces into Jordan.

Since Iraq had refused to sign an armistice agreement, she was still at war with us. An incursion into Jordan by a state hostile to Israel (in this case Iraq) would undermine the *status quo* in the Middle East and constitute a violation of Article I of the Israel-Jordan Armistice Agreement. We respected the *status quo*, but observance of the agreement depended on its not being violated by a foreign and hostile country, and we would reserve freedom of action if the *status quo* was altered.

With regard to our policy outside the Middle East, we had adopted a series of measures to strengthen our links with various states and we made special efforts to establish friendships with the peoples of Asia and Africa, which were becoming a factor of ever-growing importance in international affairs.

People often say that we are isolated. In a certain sense we are a very isolated people, by virtue of our origins, our

113

history, and our status in this region and in the world. But our roots go down deep into the soil of history. In those eventful days we were a young republic, less than nine years old; for nearly 2,000 years we had lacked sovereignty, apart from a brief interlude in Bar-Kochba's time; most of our population were immigrants from a variety of origins and with a babel of tongues. Egypt, on the other hand, had a continuous history of at least 6,000 years, and her literature went back as far. But, while neither Nasser nor his people could speak the language in which Pharaoh had addressed Joseph, and only a handful of Egyptians could comprehend the ancient writings of their land, we spoke, once again, the language our forefathers had used in their first contact with Egypt about 3,500 years ago, and our Book of Books, after 3,000 years, was still the source of our learning. Moreover, as I reminded the Knesset, like other small nations, we had our friends and well-wishers. We profited from international support, both political and material.

Some countries acquire friends easily; they are great and powerful, in control of rich and extensive areas, and have huge populations. Others acquire friends through a common religion or language, like the Arabs, Latin Americans, or Scandinavians. Others, again, form an alliance against a common enemy or other object of fear. Israel has neither wealth, power, nor territories. She shares no common language or religion with any other state. Those closest to us from the point of view of language and race are the Arabs, who, for reasons of contemporary history, are our bitterest enemies—though I believe these reasons will prove only temporary.

On what basis, then, could we, in our time of crisis, win friends? Some Jewish communities could serve as a bridge between Israel and the countries they lived in, but

114

this did not apply everywhere. In some places—almost all the countries of Asia and central Africa—the Jews were too few in number to constitute a public factor. In truth there was only one way for us to gain friends and allies: through our own creative and liberating achievements. In place of the common language, religion, or material inducements which served to create alliances between other nations, we would offer our friendship on the basis of common values and interests and our desire to share them for mutual benefit. Any endeavor of ours that was "a light to the nations" would be our emissary, winning sympathy, friendship, and good will for Israel.

Our people had always been surrounded by tension, in its own land, in exile, and even now that it had returned to the Homeland—a tension that would not speedily pass away, for it was rooted deep in history. More than any other people, we had been surrounded by suspicion, dislike, and hostility. However, we were not alone, not excommunicated. How else could we account for the generous help, and not only from America, which we had enjoyed since the establishment of the State and even before?

Many harsh things were said in our Parliament about the United Nations, but I reminded the House that, however proper her complaints, Israel must regard the United Nations as a great institution of mankind, a hope for the future of world peace. We were interested more than any other nation in protecting its moral authority, and we had implicit faith that the day would come when, in the fullness of its strength, it would establish a universal reign of peace and justice.

In Chapter 85 of the Book of Psalms we find the words: "Mercy and truth are met together: Righteousness and peace have kissed each other." President Eisenhower had said that peace and justice are indivisible. And I would add: peace without justice cannot endure. A country that did not actively protect its sovereignty, its security, and its rights would not long preserve any of them.

A few days after I had given the Knesset this survey of the general situation, new parliamentary elections took place in Jordan, the result of which, contrived by Egyptian agents using plentiful bribery, was a pro-Nasser majority. Immediately afterwards, on October 23, a tripartite military alliance was concluded between Egypt, Syria, and Jordan, which in timing was meant to frustrate certain plans of the Iraqi Government to ally its country with Jordan, and in purpose left no room for doubt: that purpose was the destruction of the State of Israel.

Chapter Eight
Operation Sinai

A glance at the map of Israel will clearly indicate the dangers to which we were exposed after Egypt, Jordan, and Syria were allied and their armies were united under Egyptian command. By a surprise attack, the Jordanian army could cut our territory in two, for the narrow strip which is the center of Israel is no more than twelve miles wide. The Syrian and Egyptian air forces could arrive at Israel's centers of population in a few minutes and, by bombarding them, prevent the mobilization of the reserves, the foundation of our entire defense. A sudden combined attack by the three countries, under a unified Egyptian command, could thus leave us entirely defenseless.

The time had come for action.

On October 27, 1956, I submitted a proposal and a plan for Operation Sinai to all the members of the Cabinet, one party at a time. Only two of the Ministers opposed it, but they stated that if the plan was adopted, they would share full responsibility for the operation. The next day, at a meeting of the full Cabinet, the plan was again discussed and approved. On October 29 I invited the leaders of the opposition parties (except for the Communists) to meet me. Informed of the plan and the Government's decision, they also gave their willing approval.

With the agreement of the Knesset Foreign Affairs and Security Committee, I had issued an order two days earlier for the mobilization of the reserves under the terms of paragraph 8 of the Defense Service Law. The response to the order was immediate. Even those who had not, for economic, educational, or administrative reasons, been called upon to report came forward voluntarily in large numbers and asked to be recruited.

The entire country thought that we were facing operations in the east, in Jordan, for Iraqi forces had already entered eastern Jordan. Reserve battalions were sent up to protect the eastern border against any sudden inroad by Jordan or Syria or both. A much larger complement of reserves was sent down to our southern borders. There was, of course, a fundamental organizational difference between our defense forces and the Arab armies: the whole Arab military potential was constantly mobilized and consisted entirely of regulars, whereas ours was built mainly on reserves, our regulars being employed principally to absorb and train recruits and to be on sentry duty at various depots.

As our mobilization was beginning, I received two messages from the President of the United States expressing his concern. In my reply of October 29, I reminded him of his constant efforts for peace in the region during the past year, which we had supported by every means in our power. It was Nasser who had frus-

118

trated any attempt for peace. I ended my letter to the President with the following analysis of our situation:

> With Iraqi troops poised on the Iraq-Jordan frontier; with the creation of the joint command of Egypt, Syria and Jordan; with the decisive increase of Egyptian influence in Jordan; and with the renewal of incursions into Israel territory by Egyptian gangs, my Government would be failing in its essential duty if it were not to take all necessary measures to ensure that the declared Arab aim of eliminating Israel by force should not come about. My Government has appealed to the people to combine alertness with calm. I feel confident that with your vast military experience you appreciate to the full the crucial danger in which we find ourselves.

In my meeting with the Cabinet the day before, I had described my plan as an extensive operation in all parts of the Sinai Desert and in the Gaza Strip. The aim was to demolish the bases of the *fedayun* and the Egyptian army in these areas and to occupy the shore of the Gulf of Aqaba so that we might safeguard freedom of navigation to and from Eilat via the Red Sea and the Indian Ocean. Egypt maintained significant military forces and military airfields in Sinai and the Gaza Strip; we would need a large force.

I was asked about the fate of Sinai if our offensive should succeed and we were to destroy all the enemy forces in the area. To this I replied:

> I do not know what will be the fate of Sinai if that should happen. We are interested first of all in the shore

119

of Eilat and the Straits. I can imagine that if we should occupy Sinai, certain forces would compel us to evacuate. There is America, there is Russia, there is the U.N., there is Nehru, there are Asia and Africa, and I am more concerned about America than about the rest. America will compel us to leave. But the main thing for us is freedom of navigation. We have, indeed, an emotional attitude to Yotvat (Tiran). But I am prepared to give that up. That is not the main thing. The main thing is that even if we are not there, we should have freedom of navigation.

One of the Ministers then asked what would be the fate of the Gaza Strip. To this I replied: "Gaza is an 'embarrassing' objective, and would be a burden for us."

The action was to begin in the evening of October 29 and to be limited to the Sinai area, without crossing the Suez Canal or touching the territory of Egypt proper. Our mobilized forces would be directed mainly to Sinai, although it would be necessary to keep a few brigades along the borders of Jordan and Syria in case their forces should go into action on orders of the Egyptian Supreme Commander. Everything would be done on our part to prevent a breach of the peace on the borders with Jordan and Syria. Our initiative would be limited entirely to the Sinai area and the Gaza Strip.

As arranged, the offensive was opened on the evening of October 29. The initial operations went according to plan and were uniquely successful. What this means can be imagined, perhaps, when it is realized that our fighters were reservists for the most part, who until four days before, had been civilians: farmers, workers, students, shopkeepers, and road builders.

About three Egyptian divisions faced us: one in the

Gaza Strip; a second in the El Arish and Abu Ageila area on the northern border of the Sinai Peninsula, just south of the Gaza Strip; and a third consisting of units scattered all over the Sinai Peninsula. From Ras el Naqb on the Egyptian border just opposite Eilat, this third division was stationed north along the border at Thamed, Kuntilla, and Kuseima; then west at Jebel Libni; and then all the way down the peninsula again at Nakhl, Tur, Ras Nasrani, and Sharm el-Sheikh at the tip of the peninsula on the Gulf of Aqaba, next to the Straits of Tiran.

The total strength, with ancillary services, of the Egyptian forces was over 30,000 men. Large reinforcements, more than two brigades numbering about 10,000 men, came up during the fighting. This combined powerful force was armed with hundreds of Soviet and British tanks, large numbers of first-class armored vehicles, and heavy artillery of all kinds. It was supported by an air force equipped with British Vampire and Meteor jet planes and Soviet Migs and Ilyushins. The Egyptian navy also went into action and an Egyptian destroyer reached Haifa port, where, after a brief engagement, it was captured by the Israeli navy.

On the first night of Operation Sinai, our forces took Kuseima, Kuntilla, and Ras el Naqb. On the next day, Thamad, El-Bassup and El-Ufard in the heart of Sinai were taken. On October 31 Bir-Hasna in central Sinai was taken despite resistance, and Nakhl, a fortified position, was also gained. Abu Ageila fell after a stiff engagement on November 1, and all the positions guarding the approaches to Rafah, in the Gaza Strip, were captured in about two hours. The approaches to El Arish and El Gafgafa on the Nitzana-Ismailiya highway were also cleared.

In the early morning of November 2, El Arish was taken after bitter resistance, and three hours later Gaza surrendered without opposition. The strongest resistance was shown at Khan Yunis, which lies between Gaza and Rafa in the Strip.

On November 3, several important posts on the western coast of the Gulf of Aqaba, including Dahab and Ras Nasrani, were occupied. The whole of the peninsula was then in effect in our hands, except for Sharm el-Sheikh, which was well fortified with long-range guns and had an airstrip. This last Egyptian stronghold in Sinai fell into our hands on the morning of November 5.

This matter-of-fact account hardly does justice to an amazing performance by young soldiers, in the main untried. Our success was not haphazard. In our planning, we had kept in mind two principal objectives: speed of action and a minimum of casualties. With profound satisfaction I learned that our successes had exceeded all expectations.

The first day, October 30, a paratroop brigade was in action driving westward through Sinai toward the Suez Canal at its southern end, where it flows into the Gulf of Suez. One battalion of the brigade had been airdropped just east of the decisive and hazardous Mitla Pass, which is in high, rocky, difficult country about 150 miles from our frontier and not more than 40 miles from Port Tewfik, at the eastern end of the Canal. The rest of the brigade had to push westward, by vehicle, through typical desert sand, in which their vehicles often sank axle-deep, and along the beds of stony wadis.

Clearing the strongly fortified Egyptian positions at Kuntilla, Thamad and Nakhl, directly in the rear of Mitla, the battalion had to leave a force at the Nakhl crossroads in case the Egyptians should send down a relief column from one of the main bases to the north and east. Nakhl, a base from which *fedayun* raiders had harassed our

"The greatest occasion in the life of our people." David Ben-Gurion
proclaiming the independence of the State of Israel in Tel Aviv
on May 14, 1948.

"There had been no public announcement of our intention, but the
news had spread and the streets were thronged with people."
Tel Aviv, May 14, 1948. The sign reads, 'The Israel Defense Forces—
To Independence, To Freedom, To Victory!"

Chaim Weizmann, distinguished Zionist and the first President of Israel.

a map of Israel showing its
ndaries and neighbors.

Mr. Ben-Gurion with President Truman and Ambassador Abba Eban
in the White House in May, 1949.

Izhak Ben-Zvi, an old friend and colleague of David Ben-Gurion, was the President of Israel until his death on April 23, 1963.

David Ben-Gurion as seen at Sdeh Boker.

"Golda Myerson conveyed to me the request of the Prime Minister, Moshe Sharett, that I should re-enter active politics and return to the post of Minister of Defense."

Two views of Sdeh Boker, where Mr. Ben-Gurion lived and worked from December, 1953, to early in 1955.

ABOVE LEFT: An Arabic translation of *Mein Kampf,* found on a number of Egyptian officers during the Sinai Campaign.

ABOVE RIGHT: A member of the Israel Defense Forces on guard ten miles from Ismailiya on November 3, 1956. The Suez Canal is in the background.

OPERATION SINAI: Gaza in Israeli hands in December, 1956.

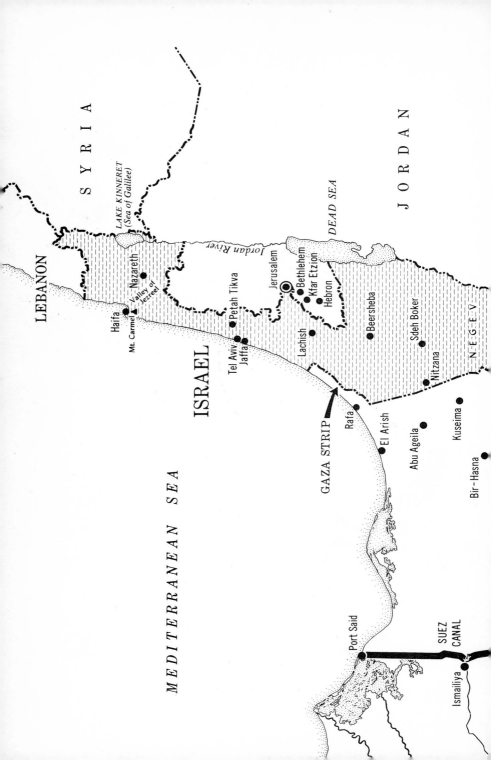

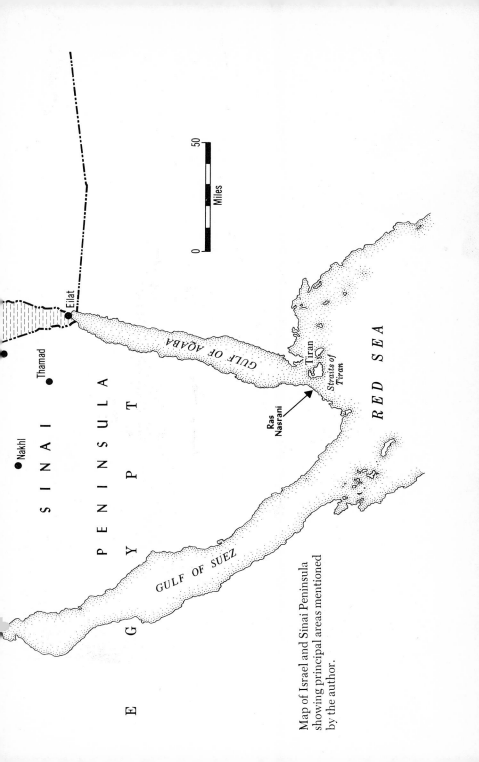

Map of Israel and Sinai Peninsula showing principal areas mentioned by the author.

E G Y P T

SINAI

PENINSULA

EGYPT

• Nakhl

• Thamad

Eilat

GULF OF AQABA

GULF OF SUEZ

Ras Nasrani

Tiran

Straits of Tiran

RED SEA

0   50

Miles

Israeli soldiers inspecting captured Egyptian tanks.

Egyptian spoils on the Sinai Peninsula.

Ibrahim-al-Awwal, an Egyptian destroyer captured on
October 31, 1956.

David Ben-Gurion and the then
chief of staff, General Moshe Dayan,
inspecting guard at Sharm-el-Sheikh.

General Burns and General Dayan at a press conference on the withdrawal from Sharm el-Sheikh and the Gaza Strip in March, 1957.

President Ben-Zvi, Prime Minister Ben-Gurion, and General Dayan review the Israel Defense Forces on the first Independence Day after the Sinai Campaign.

A general view of the port at Eilat in March, 1960.

Mr. and Mrs. Ben-Gurion having breakfast with Dag Hammarskjöld at Sdeh Boker in January, 1959.

David Ben-Gurion with President Eisenhower in March, 1960.

countryside, was captured and a small force of our earth-bound paratroopers was left there to guard the cross-roads; the rest jogged on. That night, at about ten-thirty, the weary paratroopers, who had been turned into infantry, made contact with their air-borne comrades east of the Mitla Pass, and the brigade was ready to move to the next and perhaps most difficult stage of the operation.

Many people were puzzled by the use of the bulk of a paratroop brigade for an infantry job, when enough infantry regiments were available for the operation. I cannot do better than repeat the official army explanation:

The overland route to the forward position known as Parker's Memorial, east of the Mitla Pass, was hard and hazardous. The distance is 125 miles and the track could not be expected to take the weight of the number of vehicles, many of them tracked, needed to move an infantry brigade to schedule. Taking all this into account, it was considered advisable, as a means of making doubly sure of the junction with the parachute battalion dropped at Parker's Memorial, that a special psychological link should exist between the column moving overland and the battalion towards which it was moving, a link that would accentuate the urge to surmount all obstacles, expected and unexpected: the bond of a mother-formation with one of its own units.

And so it proved. The casualties of the paratroop brigade had been few, although a good many vehicles had had to be abandoned during the thirty wearing hours the operation had taken before junction was made. Mine-fields had been successfully negotiated. The attackers at

Thamad and Nakhl had met with resistance, but the Egyptians, taken by surprise, had been in poor heart. Now, however, ahead of the paratroop brigade rose the massive and easily defensible Mitla Pass, which was expected to offer sharp resistance. And behind it, the first of Colonel Nasser's new Migs were preparing to take off. The Egyptians had also dispatched an armored column across the Canal, which was now making in the direction of Parker's Memorial.

Meanwhile, northwestwards, an infantry brigade had advanced upon and captured the key road junction of Kuseima, taking prisoners and sending off a column down the seventy miles of track and drift sand to join up with the paratroop unit which had been left to defend the Nakhl junction. Simultaneously, an armored brigade had been in action well to the west. Indeed, within thirty hours of the opening of our offensive, the main forces of our field army had broken through most of the forward positions of the Egyptian army and were poised for the breakthrough to Ismailiya, on the Suez Canal, and for the daring assault on Nasser's major bases and army concentrations at El Arish and Rafa, on the northwestern coast of the peninsula and just east of the Gaza Strip.

Everything had gone wonderfully well, but it had been a tense thirty hours. Every operation had been carefully worked out, but there was always the risk of some unforeseen hazard. I was greatly relieved, for example, when I received the message stating that the parachutists had been successfully dropped at Parker's Memorial and had met with no interference from Egyptian aircraft. I had been worried, too, about possible Egyptian reaction in the form of air raids on the civilian population. After all, Egypt had more than 100 Mig-15's, 50 Ilyushin fighter bombers able to carry two tons each, and a num-

ber of Vampires and Meteors. I had given orders that
our aircraft should not pass beyond the Suez Canal into
Egypt proper or attack enemy cities. Also, they were not
to operate against enemy ground troops or to fire on enemy aircraft. I had given these orders because the action
we had felt compelled to launch was not, in my calcula-
tions, full-scale war. I had planned that it should be
swift and purposeful, the purpose being to insure, at least
for a period, a stable frontier and the rights of navigation, if not through the Suez Canal then at least to and
from Eilat by way of the Red Sea and the Straits of Tiran.
I had feared that aerial fighting might lead to total warfare and that, in turn, to an extension of hostilities going
even as far as another world war.

That first night, Tel Aviv and other towns were blacked
out, but the Egyptian bombers did not come. Ill at the
time, I was at my house in Tel Aviv and my sickroom had
become my office; there I was compelled to transact the
urgent business of Prime Minister, Minister of Defense,
and Commander-in-Chief. Thanks to the good humor and
tirelessness of Ministers, staff officers, secretaries, and the
rest, and the constant care and watchfulness of my wife
Paula, my illness was not the inconvenience it might
have been.

On Tuesday morning, October 31, at 9 A.M., I was able
to authorize the publication of our first communiqué. It
read:

"Israel forces have struck into the heart of Sinai and
are more than halfway to Suez."

That evening I received a warning that we would be
getting an ultimatum from the British Government calling upon us to keep our troops from approaching nearer
than ten miles to the banks of the Suez Canal. A similar
ultimatum was on the way to the Egyptian Government.

125

We had no particular desire to straddle the Suez Canal and I was not perturbed by the prospect of such an ultimatum.

Meanwhile, our parachute brigade was assembling before the Mitla Pass and preparing for battle. The battle began at noon the following day. The Mitla defile is bow-shaped, steep, rocky, and about four miles long. There was no indication at the time of the strength with which it was held, but as soon as our forces moved into the pass, they found themselves up against strong positions of ambush along the top of the cliffs and in concealed caves. The parachutists came under devastating fire from positions they could not see, and at the same time were attacked by four Mig fighters, which, however, were driven off soon afterwards by two of our own fighters. The battle lasted seven hours and in some respects was the hardest fought of the whole campaign. Some of the Egyptians escaped; others were taken prisoner.

At about midnight on October 30 the full terms of the British ultimatum, requiring Israel and Egyptian forces to make no military move within ten miles of the Suez Canal banks, was received. We had had no intention of occupying the Canal, and certainly none of crossing it into Egypt proper. It was not difficult, therefore, to accept the ultimatum. We learned on the morning of October 31 that the Egyptians had rejected the ultimatum. Later in the day, I was informed that British and French fighter and bomber aircraft were in action against the Egyptians on the south bank of the Canal and were attacking Egyptian airfields. Naturally I was relieved to learn that the Egyptians would be unable to carry out bomber raids against our cities and towns.

Whatever might be happening at Port Said, where Anglo-French forces were said to be concentrating, or

among the Egyptian airfields on the other side of the
Canal, our objective remained the same: destruction of
the major Egyptian bases at El Arish and Rafah, on the
peninsula's Mediterranean coast to the north, and on the
coastal road to Kantara, between Port Said and Ismailiya; the capture of Abu Ageila, commanding the desert
road to Ismailiya, on the Canal; the clearing of the road
leading from the Mitla Pass to the Canal at its entry into
the Gulf of Suez, which leads to the Red Sea; and, in my
reckoning almost most important of all, the occupation
of the southern tip of the peninsula at Sharm el-Sheikh
and the clearing of the way from the Red Sea through
the Gulf of Aqaba to Eilat.

Abu Ageila fell after a stiff engagement on November
1, and the way was thus open for the decisive northern
offensive against Rafa. It began at 0400 hours that day
with the attack on Rafa's fortified approaches. After the
first breakthrough, the Chief of Staff, Major-General
Moshe Dayan, appeared on the front line and gave the
order for the final attack. At three o'clock that afternoon the assault was launched. The battle was hard, but
it was over by nightfall. Our forces were in the key position of Rafa, part of them already moving in the direction of Kantara and the Suez Canal at the Port Said end,
and another part in the opposite direction toward Khan
Yunis, just inside the Gaza Strip. By that night we were
in full possession of the three lines of communication
leading through Sinai from west to east, that is to say,
from the peninsula where it comes up against the southern borders of Israel to the Suez Canal. The whole of the
Egyptian chain of command had broken down.

Vast stores of fuel, food, and clothing, and a massive
booty of Czechoslovak and Russian tanks, guns, vehicles,
and electronic equipment had fallen into our hands. We

had taken more prisoners than were convenient to handle, and for the rest, a disorganized group of Egyptian soldiers were plodding wearily through sand dunes toward the Canal. Next morning, November 2, we captured El Arish. Khan Yunis had fallen after a sharp battle, and that day the Egyptian command of the Gaza Strip surrendered. Our columns were swinging down to within ten miles of the canal, in the Kantara area. Further columns were moving along the main desert highway from Abu Ageila to within ten miles of the Canal facing Ismailiya. Colonel Sharon's parachute brigade, which had gained the Mitla Pass, was already within ten miles of the Canal at its Port Said end. We were now in position along the whole length of the Canal, and all the Sinai Peninsula was ours except that vital tip, the peninsula proper, which commanded the sea passage through the Straits of Tiran.

The operation here was characteristic of the whole Sinai Campaign, of the hardihood and resource of our men, their excellent leadership and their determination to carry out the task set them as nearly as possible to the allotted time schedule. The brigade engaged on this hazardous enterprise was under the command of the bulky Colonel Avraham Yoffe, who had distinguished himself in the War of Independence. His men, farmers for the most part, had been mobilized on Friday, October 26, and had had to make their way from the fields and villages north and west of Haifa to the assembly point at Kfar Yeroham, about forty miles into the desert beyond Beersheba.

Their route into battle lay through some of the most difficult, trackless sands and sharp, rocky ridges in Sinai. They had to mount three thousand feet of sharp-edged,

128

sun-heated stone; they had to plod through rolling hills of sand; a little farther along, they had to shift huge boulders blocking defiles and worm their way through the twisting, bruising passage to an opening leading on to what looked like trackless moon-country. By November 1 they had reached Ras el Naqb, west of Eilat at the head of the Gulf of Aqaba, where they received orders to halt for twenty-four hours until the battle for Rafa, in the north, was begun and the responsible commanders would be in a position to release aircraft in support of Colonel Yoffe's brigade if that should be necessary.

On the eve of November 3 the brigade reached Dahab, on the Gulf, and engaged in a short skirmish with a small Egyptian garrison. A motor torpedo boat, which had been carried overland from Haifa to the port of Eilat, came into Dahab with fuel for the brigade, which then pushed on to what should have been its decisive battle at Ras Nasrani. This was a large, jutting rock with four powerful naval guns mounted on it and a veritable fortress-barracks, hewn out of the rock, capable of lodging a regiment. It was surrounded by concrete bunkers, wire entanglements, and a broad apron of minefields.

However, the Egyptians, after destroying their guns, had already moved out by the time Colonel Yoffe's brigade arrived. It became clear that the garrison had gone down the peninsula to take up position with the smaller Sharm el-Sheikh garrison, which was also the administrative center of the region. The brigade, making use of the asphalt road, reached Sharm el-Sheikh on November 5 and at once assaulted the Egyptian lines. The breakthrough came quickly, and within a few hours the garrison had surrendered. Colonel Yoffe's brigade rested thirty hours at Sharm el-Sheikh. They had accomplished their task magnificently, and we were in control of the Straits leading from the Red Sea through the Gulf of Aqaba to Eilat.

The brigade, consisting of men who had been interrupted at the sowing of their winter crops and the picking of their ripened fruit, were ordered to return home and attend to their farms as soon as the thirty hours' rest had been completed. Having traveled fourteen hundred miles to Sharm el-Sheikh and back, they had covered some of the most difficult terrain to be found anywhere in the Middle East. The Egyptians had been dumbfounded. It had seemed to them against all reason that a hostile force should descend upon them over a hazardous land barrier, their natural and unapproachable defense.

The Sinai Campaign was over. The entire operation had taken one week. Our losses had been few in relation to the magnitude of the campaign and the size and strength of the forces confronting us. Against Egypt's three divisions, numbering, with ancillary services, over 30,000 men, and later reinforced by two brigades numbering in all about 10,000 men, we had put nine brigades into Sinai, of which all but one were used in combat. Our brigade, however, is not equivalent in numbers to a brigade of the United States Army but is closer to a United States regiment at peacetime strength.

Military historians of the future will doubtless make thorough studies of the secret of this brief operation, conducted in a vast area of desert against an enemy armed and equipped down to the smallest detail with the finest modern weapons. In its mopping-up operations, our army discovered at first hand the astonishing quantity and excellence of the heavy armaments that Czechoslovakian manufacturers had been supplying to Egypt. It was only after the occupation of the Gaza Strip, Abu Ageila, El

Arish, Nakhl, Mitla near the western border of the peninsula, and the Straits of Tiran that we became fully aware
of the massive quantity and up-to-date quality of
Egypt's tanks and guns, to say nothing of communications equipment, motor transport, armored vehicles, clothing, and supplies, all more numerous and far better than
anything we had.

The enormous amount of Egyptian armaments now
in our hands proved once and for all that Nasser had
squeezed Egypt's hungry masses to the limit to provide
the army, on which his rule rested, with abundant supplies and luxurious living. Nor is it strange that among
the Egyptian officers' equipment left behind in the desert
we found an Arabic translation of Hitler's *Mein Kampf*.

All their modern arms availed not the Egyptians, for
in them there was no spirit. The words of Isaiah were fulfilled:

The Lord hath mingled within her
A spirit of dizziness;
And they have caused Egypt to stagger in every work
thereof,
As a drunken man staggereth in his vomit.
(Isaiah 19:14)

After 3,300 years, we were at Mount Sinai again. The
peninsula and the Gaza Strip were rid of the plague of
the Egyptians, from Ras el Naqb opposite Eilat, south to
Sharm el-Sheikh at the tip of the peninsula; and from
the Eilat-Rafa line in the north to the Suez Canal and its
southern outlet, a stretch of 24,000 square miles, three
times as large as Israel. This was one of the finest military
campaigns in Jewish history.

The Israel Defense Forces had again proved their skill

and valor, and the world, no less than Jewry in Israel and the Diaspora, acclaimed them generously. In a week of lightning advances they had done away with the *fedayun* and their bases, and for the time being had effectively scotched Nasser's offensive plans. The entire nation expressed its admiration and affection for the men who had so powerfully reinforced the security of Israel.

The army had also led us back to the highest point of our history, to the spot where the Law was given according to local tradition and we were enjoined to be a chosen people. We saw come to life again the eternal verses telling of the departure from Egypt and the coming of our forefathers to the desert.

> And when they were departed from Rephidim, and were come to the wilderness of Sinai, they encamped in the wilderness; and there Israel encamped before the mount. And Moses went up unto God, and the Lord called unto him out of the mountain, saying: "Thus shalt thou say to the house of Jacob, and tell the children of Israel: Ye have seen what I did unto the Egyptians, and how I bore you on eagles' wings, and brought you unto Myself. Now therefore, if ye will hearken unto My voice indeed, and keep My covenant, then ye shall be Mine own treasure from among all peoples; for all the earth is Mine. . . ." (Exodus 19: 2-5)

On November 7, I gave Parliament an account of the Sinai Campaign and discussed our prospects for the future. There were several issues, I told them, on which we would have to make our stand clear immediately in the eyes of the world.

First, the Armistice Agreement with Egypt was dead,

132

buried, and could not be restored to life. Nasser had made of it a harmful fiction, serving only his destructive designs. To return to it meant a return to murder, boy= cott, and blockade, aimed at our destruction.

Second, like the agreement, the Armistice lines be- tween Israel and Egypt had lost their validity.

Third, we had no dispute with the people of Egypt. It was Nasser who had brought catastrophe upon them by inciting them to war against us.

Fourth, we did not want our relations with Egypt to continue in a state of anarchy. We were ready to negoti- ate for a stable peace and co-operation, provided that the negotiations were direct, without prior conditions on either side, and under no duress from any quarter. We hoped that all the peace-loving nations would support us in this desire.

Fifth, we were prepared for such negotiations with each of the other Arab states; if they refused, then so long as they observed the Armistice Agreements, Israel for her part would do so, too.

Sixth, on no account would Israel agree to the presence of a foreign force, by whatever name, in her territory or in any areas she occupied.

X Seventh, Israel would not fight against Egypt or any other Arab country unless first attacked.

Such were the principles of our policy for the stormy days we knew were ahead. I concluded my review in the Knesset with these words:

> It is possible that a difficult political struggle awaits us, and perhaps something more grave. We have had difficult trials to bear in the past and we have not re- coiled. We shall not imitate the futile arrogance of the Arab rulers, but we shall not humble ourselves before

the powerful forces of the world when right is not on their side. In our efforts to bring peace and justice to this part of the world we look for the support of all men of good will and lovers of peace among all nations. Let us meet the days ahead with courage and wisdom, conscious of our strength and the justice of our cause, without ignoring our natural and necessary ties with the world family of nations.

Chapter Nine
The Aftermath

The stormy days we had anticipated were not slow in coming. I have already touched upon the first indication of Anglo-French intervention against Egypt: the British ultimatum to Israel and Egypt, received on the night of October 30, requiring that Egyptian and Israeli forces remain at least ten miles from the banks of the Suez Canal and withdraw that distance from the Canal if already within the proscribed area. We immediately agreed to this demand, while Egypt rejected it out of hand. On October 31, after a further warning, Anglo-French air forces began to bombard Port Said and the airfields on the other side of the Canal. The Security Council of the United Nations immediately assembled.

The United States submitted a severe motion of censure against Britain, France, and Israel. Britain and France imposed a veto on this resolution. The majority in the Council thereupon convened an emergency session of the General Assembly, which, on November 2, called upon all belligerents to cease fire and upon all members of the United Nations to withhold further arms supplies to the countries involved.

The Assembly also adopted two further resolutions. The first demanded that Britain and France should evacuate their forces from Egyptian territory, and that Israel should withdraw her forces behind the demarcation lines laid down in the Armistice Agreement of 1949. The second resolution provided for the establishment of a United Nations Emergency Force. The Emergency Assembly decided to continue in session until these resolutions had been observed.

On November 3, the Government of Israel announced that it agreed to the cease-fire. At the Assembly, the Israel Ambassador, Mr. Abba Eban, explained the background and the motives of the Sinai Campaign, and his address aroused much sympathy for Israel.

On November 5, I received the following letter from Marshal N. Bulganin, then President of the Council of Ministers of the Soviet Union:

Mr. Prime Minister,

The Soviet Government has already expressed its unqualified condemnation of the armed aggression of Israel, as well as of Britain and France, against Egypt, which constitutes a direct and open violation of the Charter and the principles of the United Nations. At the special Emergency Session of the Assembly, the great majority of the countries of the world have also condemned the act of aggression that was perpetrated on the Egyptian Republic and called on the governments of Israel, Britain, and France to put an end to the military operations without delay, and to withdraw the invading armies from Egyptian territory. The whole of

136

peace-loving humanity indignantly condemns the criminal acts of the aggressors who have violated the territorial integrity, the sovereignty, and the independence of the Egyptian Republic.

Without taking this into account, the Government of Israel, acting as an instrument of external imperialistic forces, perseveres in the senseless adventure, thus defying all the peoples of the East who are conducting a struggle against colonialism and for their freedom and independence, and all peace-loving peoples in the world.

These acts of the Government of Israel clearly demonstrate the value to be attached to all its false declarations about Israel's love of peace and her aspirations to peaceful coexistence with the neighboring Arab countries. In these declarations the Government of Israel in effect aimed only at dulling the vigilance of the other peoples, while she prepared a treacherous attack on her neighbors in obedience to a foreign will and acting according to orders from without.

The Government of Israel is criminally and irresponsibly playing with the fate of the world, with the fate of its own people. It is sowing hatred of the State of Israel among the Eastern peoples, such as cannot but leave its mark on the future of Israel as a State. Vitally interested in the maintenance of peace and the preservation of tranquillity in the Middle East, the Soviet Government is at this moment taking steps to put an end to the war and to restrain the aggressors.

We propose that the Government of Israel should consider, before it is too late, and should put an end to her military measures against Egypt. We appeal to you, to the Parliament, to the workers of the Israel State, to all the people of Israel: Stop the aggression! Stop the bloodshed! Withdraw your armies from Egyptian territory.

In view of the situation that has been created, the Soviet Government has decided to ask its Ambassador in Tel Aviv to leave Israel and set out for Moscow without delay. We hope that the Government of Israel will fully understand and appreciate this warning of ours.

N. BULGANIN

On November 8, a letter from the President of the United States was received, more friendly in tone but firmly demanding a withdrawal to the Armistice lines. President Eisenhower wrote:

Dear Mr. Prime Minister,

As you know, the General Assembly of the United Nations has arranged a cease-fire in Egypt to which Egypt, France, the United Kingdom, and Israel have agreed. There is being dispatched to Egypt a United Nations force in accordance with pertinent resolutions of the General Assembly. That body has urged that all other foreign forces be withdrawn from Egyptian territory, and especially, that Israel forces be withdrawn to the General Armistice line. The resolution covering the cease-fire and withdrawal was introduced by the United States and received the overwhelming vote of the Assembly.

Statements attributed to your Government to the effect that Israel does not intend to withdraw from Egyptian territory, as requested by the United Nations, have been called to my attention.

I must say frankly, Mr. Prime Minister, that the United States views these reports, if true, with deep concern. Any such decision by the Government of Israel would seriously undermine the urgent efforts being made by the United Nations to restore peace in the Middle East, and could not but bring about the condemnation of Israel as a violator of the principles as well as the directives of the United Nations.

It is our belief that as a matter of highest priority, peace should be restored and foreign troops, except for United Nations forces, withdrawn from Egypt, after which new and energetic steps should be undertaken within the framework of the United Nations to solve the basic problems which have given rise to the present difficulty. The United States has tabled in the General Assembly two resolutions designed to accomplish the latter purposes and hopes that they will be acted upon favorably as soon as the present emergency has been dealt with.

I need not assure you of the deep interest which the United States has in your country, nor recall the various elements of our policy of support to Israel in so many ways. It is in this context that I urge you to comply with the Resolutions of the United Nations General Assembly dealing with the current crisis and to make your decision known immediately. It would be a matter of the greatest regret to all my countrymen if Israeli policy on a matter of such grave concern to the world should in any way impair the friendly co-operation between our two countries.

With best wishes,

Sincerely,

DWIGHT D. EISENHOWER

On November 9, two meetings of the Cabinet were held, at which the replies to the letters were discussed. I also invited the leaders of all the opposition parties (except the Communists) to a meeting, informed them of what was happening in the United Nations Assembly and the world's capitals, and explained the policy adopted by the Government in replying to the two letters.

My reply to Marshal Bulganin's note pointed out the inaccuracies in the note and recapitulated the grievous tale of *fedayun* raids from Egyptian territory, which had marked the two previous years. A photostatic copy of an Egyptian Order by the Commander of the Third Egyptian Division in Sinai, setting out what every commander in the field should do to prepare "himself and his subordinates for the inevitable campaign against Israel . . . the annihilation of Israel and her extermination in the shortest possible time and in the most brutal and cruel battles," was enclosed with my reply to Marshal Bulganin. I listed Egypt's numerous contraventions of the terms of the United Nations Charter and of decisions of the Security Council, referred to the military pact between Egypt, Jordan, and Syria, and reiterated our willingness to "enter immediately into direct negotiations with Egypt to achieve a stable peace without prior conditions and without any compulsion." I could not avoid adding my surprise and sorrow at the threat against Israel's existence contained in the Marshal's note. My reply concluded with the assertion that our foreign policy was dictated by our essential needs and by our yearning for peace; it would not be decided by any foreign factor.

My reply to President Eisenhower took note of his statement that a United Nations force was being dispatched to Egypt. I welcomed this development and pointed out that neither I nor any authorized spokesman of the Government of Israel had ever declared that it was our plan to annex the Sinai Peninsula. I expressed our willingness to withdraw our forces in accordance with the pertinent United Nations resolution, upon the conclusion of satisfactory arrangements with the United Nations regarding the international force about to enter the Suez Canal area. I then pointed out that, although as a result of our operation *fedayun* bases had been destroyed, it was necessary to repeat our urgent request to the United Nations to call upon Egypt to renounce her status as a belligerent, implying war with Israel, to abandon her policy of blockade and boycott, to cease sending murder gangs into Israel territory, and to enter into direct peace negotiations with Israel. I also expressed my profound thanks for the words of friendship which had been contained in President Eisenhower's note.

Our Foreign Minister, Golda Meir, replied in a similar vein to the United Nations Secretary-General, who had transmitted to her the Assembly resolutions containing the demand for a withdrawal to the Armistice lines.

Marshal Bulganin was apparently not content with the Government of Israel's reply to his first letter, and on November 15 he sent a second, which declared that ". . . it was not the Arab governments but precisely Israel which has been guilty of many armed attacks on the territory of neighboring Arab states."

Marshal Bulganin went on: "The Security Council has expressed grave concern with regard to the non-fulfilment by the Israel Government of its obligations under the Armistice Agreement, and has called on the Israel Government to carry out these obligations in future under threat of applying suitable sanctions against Israel, as provided by the United Nations Charter."

The note complained that Israel had "not only failed to comply with the General Assembly's call for an immediate cease-fire and the withdrawal of troops which had in-

141

vaded Egypt, but has even openly announced its annexationist claims with regard to Egypt, its plans to seize and attach to Israel the Gaza Region, the Sinai Peninsula and the islands of Tiran and Sanafir in the Gulf of Aqaba."

We were told that "even when compelled to decide on the withdrawal of its troops from Egyptian territory, the Israel Government still attempts to make compliance with this demand provisional on a 'satisfactory agreement with the United Nations with regard to the entry of the international force into the Suez Canal Zone,' which, as is known, is an inalienable part of the sovereign Egyptian State."

Marshal Bulganin also claimed that, "as a result of the aggression launched against Egypt by Israel, Egyptian towns and inhabited localities have been destroyed, thousands of innocent people have been killed and maimed, and damage has been inflicted on Egyptian communications, trade, and economy. But what has Israel achieved? Only the blind can fail to see that aggression has brought nothing good to Israel either."

However, the Soviet Government understood that the Israeli Government had ceased fire and subsequently had announced the forthcoming withdrawal of Israeli troops from Egyptian territory.

Marshal Bulganin went on to say: "At the same time, in order to stabilize the situation in the Near East and to liquidate the consequences of the aggression against Egypt, the Soviet Government considers it essential that measures be undertaken which would exclude the possibilities of new provocation by Israel against neighboring states and would ensure a durable peace and tranquillity in the Near East.

"Justice also demands that Egypt, as the victim of un-

142

provoked aggression, should be compensated by Israel, as well as by Britain and France, for the losses inflicted as a result of the destruction of Egyptian towns and inhabited localities, and as a result of interruption in the operation of the Suez Canal and the destruction of its installations. In addition, Israel is obliged to return to Egypt all property which has been removed from Egyptian territory by the Israel armed forces which invaded it."

The note then declared that "The international armed forces of the United Nations, to whose creation the Egyptian Government has agreed, according to the United Nations Resolutions, must be deployed on both sides of the Demarcation Line between Israel and Egypt established by the Armistice Agreement."

And once again we were told to "draw the proper conclusions from the lessons which the latest events indicate for Israel." I replied on November 17 to Marshal Bulganin, as follows:

Mr. President of the Council of Ministers:

I have received your letter of November 15, 1956. In view of the statements contained therein, I feel compelled to draw your attention once more to the true state of affairs in the relations between Egypt and Israel, which has produced the present crisis.

The basic fact of the situation is that when the State of Israel was established on May 14, 1948, the Egyptian army, and with it the armies of the other Arab states, invaded our country for the purpose of annihilating us. Upon the termination of these hostilities Armistice Agreements were signed between Egypt, Lebanon, Jordan and Syria on the one hand, and Israel on the other. Egypt, however, did not honour her

143

obligations under these agreements and has continued her hostile acts against Israel to this day.

I cannot but express my surprise at the fact that you do not appear to be aware of these roots of the tension in our area, and I must therefore stress the true background of this situation.

The facts are as follows:

1. When the General Assembly of the United Nations in November, 1947, resolved in favour of the establishment of the Jewish State, Egypt at the head of the Arab states stated publicly that she would not recognize this solution and would oppose it.

2. Pursuant to this defiant declaration, the Egyptian army, together with the military forces of the other Arab states, invaded the State of Israel on the night of May 15, 1948, for the purpose of destroying Israel.

3. In the course of the proceedings of the Security Council after this brutal invasion the representatives of the USSR and of the Ukrainian SSR, together with the spokesmen of other states, condemned the action of Egypt and other Arab states in attacking Israel. At the 309th meeting of the Security Council on May 29, 1948, Mr. Gromyko, the representative of the USSR, stated: "Indeed, what is happening in Palestine can only be described as military operations organized by a group of states against the Jewish State," and that "the states whose forces had invaded Palestine have ignored the Security Council's resolution."

4. At the 366th meeting of the Security Council on July 14, 1948, Mr. Gromyko, the representative of the USSR, declared that "the Arabs despatched their troops to invade Palestinian territory and made no bones about informing the whole world that it was their firm inten-

tion to prevent the creation of independent Arab and Jewish states in Palestine."

5. In the armistice agreement between Israel and Egypt, signed on February 24, 1949, it was expressly stated that the purpose of the agreement was "to promote the return of permanent peace in Palestine."

6. In spite of the fact that Egypt signed this agreement, the rulers of that country have maintained ever since that Egypt is in a state of war with Israel.

7. This declaration of the Egyptian Government is contrary not merely to the terms of the Armistice Agreements, but also to the Charter of the United Nations, which requires all member states of the United Nations to live together in peace with one another as good neighbours and to adjust all international disputes by peaceful means.

8. The Security Council in its resolution of September 1951 expressly denied the right of either party to the Armistice Agreement "to assert that it is actively a belligerent." Egypt defied this decision too, and continued to proclaim that she was in a state of war with Israel.

9. As one of its instruments of war against Israel the Government of Egypt organized an economic boycott of Israel and used intimidation to apply pressure on business undertakings in various countries in order that they should break off economic relations with Israel.

10. In violation of the Constantinople Convention of 1888, which guarantees to all countries freedom of navigation in the Suez Canal in time of peace as in time of war, and in defiance of the resolution adopted by the Security Council on September 1, 1951, which prohibited interference with Israel's right of free naviga-

tion in the Suez Canal, Egypt has continued to maintain a maritime blockade against the State of Israel in the Canal.

11. On October 13, 1956, the Security Council unanimously adopted a resolution prohibiting any overt or covert discrimination against any state in regard to navigation in the Suez Canal. This was immediately followed by a renewed declaration on the part of the Egyptian Government that Israel shipping would not be allowed to pass through the Canal.

12. The Egyptian Government did not limit itself to a maritime blockade in the Suez Canal, but throughout the period under consideration extended its blockade also to the Gulf of Akaba. In violation of international law it prevented Israel shipping from passing through the Gulf on its way to and from Eilat.

13. In pursuing her war against Israel, in continuous contravention of the Armistice Agreement, Egypt did not confine herself to the maintenance of the economic boycott and the maritime blockade designed to bring about the economic collapse of our country. For the past two years the Egyptian Government has organized specially trained gangs of murderers and saboteurs, known as *fedayin,* * and sent them clandestinely from the Gaza Strip and the Sinai desert into our villages and onto our highways. These terrorist gangs have murdered Israel workers in the fields, travellers on the roads and children in the schools. They have also blown up irrigation pipes and agricultural installations in our villages.

14. We have in our possession citations issued to these murderers by officers of the Egyptian regular

* This spelling was used in the original document. Both it and *fedayun,* used in the rest of this book, are permissible.

army; files describing the itineraries and activities of the *fedayin* groups who were under the direct command of the Egyptian army in the Gaza Strip and the Sinai desert; furthermore, documents showing that these gangs received their arms and equipment from units of the Egyptian army. In my letter to you of November 8, 1956, I enclosed photostatic evidence of Egypt's design to destroy Israel. If you so desire, I shall supply you with additional photostatic evidence proving the connection between these gangs of murderers and saboteurs and the commanders of the Egyptian army.

15. The rulers of Egypt have repeatedly proclaimed throughout the last eight years—and these declarations have become more outspoken and more frequent during the past two years—that the time was drawing near when the Egyptian army would eliminate Israel by force.

Have these declarations never reached your ears?

In recent months matters have come to a head. A series of developments has brought home to us the imminent danger to our very existence:

(a) A few weeks ago Egypt signed aggressive military pacts with Syria and Jordan, the purpose of which was the destruction of Israel;

(b) During the period of the Suez crisis, when the Security Council was considering the problem of the Canal, the activities of the *fedayin* ceased. As soon, however, as the Security Council had completed its deliberations on the subject, Egypt intensified the murderous activities of these gangs. Hundreds of these trained murderers who had previously been sent by the Egyptian military command to the other Arab countries—Jordan, Syria and the Lebanon—received orders to step up their activities from these bases against Israel's citizens and border villages all along our frontiers in the north, east and south. Almost every day peaceful Israel citizens were murdered by the terror squads sent out by the Egyptian military dictator;

In the Gaza Strip and all along our borders with the Sinai peninsula, enormous Egyptian military forces were concentrated, equipped with tremendous quantities of aggressive weapons, and poised to attack and destroy Israel.

These facts are known to the entire world.

I would add that the vast quantities of Egyptian weapons and military equipment which were destroyed by our forces in the Sinai desert clearly indicate the intentions and the preparations of the Egyptian dictator.

It was therefore the elementary duty of our Government to take defensive measures in accordance with the right assured to every state under Article 51 of the Charter of the United Nations—in order to protect the lives of its citizens and defend the existence of the State by uprooting the *fedayin* nests and the Egyptian military bases which directed their activities. Any other people similarly placed would have been compelled to do the same.

You say in your letter that in my address to the Israel Parliament on November 7, 1956, I stated that the Armistice Agreements signed by Israel with the Arab states were no longer valid. This is not correct. If you examine the text of my speech you will find that I said in that address that Israel on her part will observe the Armistice Agreements with other Arab countries— even though the latter are not prepared for permanent peace—so long as they on their part are ready to observe these agreements. What I said in the Knesset was that the Armistice Agreement with Egypt—and only that with Egypt, not those with the other Arab states—is dead and buried and will not return to life. For years the Egyptian dictator has treated the Agreement with contempt, has violated its principles and purposes, has defied the Charter of the United Nations and the resolutions of the Security Council. By his repeated declarations that a state of war existed between Egypt and Israel he distorted the nature and aim of the Armistice Agreement, whose first and fundamental article states that it was signed with a view to promoting the return of permanent peace.

In my speech I stated further that "the Egyptian dictator has throughout been exploiting the Agreement as a smokescreen for his murderous attack against Israel citizens, and as a cover for his relentless blockade of Israel on land, at sea and in the air. Colonel Nasser did not content himself with the *fedayin* gangs which he organized in the territory under his control: he also directed and activated these gangs against Israel from the other Arab countries. In this way the Armistice Agreement became a harmful and a dangerous fiction, serving only the destructive plans of the Egyptian dictator. Any return to the Armistice Agreement means a return to murder, blockade and boycott, directed against Israel, aimed at her ultimate destruction.

As for the recent resolutions of the General Assembly of the United Nations, we have announced that we have ceased fire, and that we are prepared to withdraw our forces from Egypt when satisfactory arrangements have been made with the United Nations in connection with the international force mentioned in the General Assembly resolutions. This declaration remains fully valid.

From the mass flight and surrender of the Egyptian soldiers—peasants torn from their homes in Egypt and sent against their will to do battle in a remote desert—it is clear that these soldiers were not prepared to fight for the fascist dictator of Cairo. The first to flee were officers of the Egyptian army.

There is conclusive proof of the fact that many people in Egypt have come to understand the true character of Gamal Abdul Nasser, who at the beginning pretended that he was concerned to improve the conditions of his people—in health, education and economic development—but who since then has shown himself to be consumed by the lust of power and the ambition to impose his rule on all the Islamic peoples. He has squandered his country's resources to increase his military power and his armaments in order to carry through his expansionist ambitions and make himself master of the Moslem world.

I have to point out that your statements regarding our military operations are not accurate. We have not destroyed a single Egyptian town, nor have we caused harm to any civilian centre. We have not damaged the Suez Canal; as far as we know, the Canal has been blocked by the Egyptians themselves. Our forces were given strict instructions not to injure civilians, and these instructions were faithfully observed. The transport which did suffer—and this for years—was that of Israel, in the air, on land and at sea, as a result of Egypt's illegal blockade. If there is a case for claiming compensation it is we who are entitled to compensation for the Egyptian invasion of our country in 1947, for the deaths of thousands of our sons and daughters as a result of this aggression, for the economic boycott and the maritime blockade maintained in defiance of the UN Charter and the Security Council's resolutions, for the hundreds of Israelis, Jews and Arabs, murdered by the *fedayin,* and for all the damage caused to our economy, running into millions of pounds. However, if peace is established between Egypt and ourselves, we shall be ready to forgive all past transgressions of the Egyptian rulers.

In closing, I would repeat my statement that, in accordance with Article 33 of the U.N. Charter, Israel is prepared for a settlement of her dispute with Egypt, as well as with other Arab states, by peaceful means. It is with regret that I have to point out that several of the expressions on Israel used in your letter are not likely to be interpreted by the Arab rulers as an encouragement to the achievement of peace in our region. Nor would they appear appropriate to the accepted relations between states members of the United Nations.

I am confident that if the USSR will lend its support to bring about direct peace negotiations between Israel and her neighbours, this will be a real and significant contribution to the strengthening of peace in the Middle East and throughout the world.

D. BEN-GURION

The controversy in which Israel was engaged at that time was not only with the Soviet Union but with the entire United Nations Organization, and in the first place with the Government of the United States. In the course of this controversy, wihch lasted till the beginning of March, Israel had the opportunity to enlighten world public opinion on the motives that had led her to carry out the Sinai operation—which she had been unable to do, of course, before the campaign. The valor of the Israel Defense Forces in this campaign, much more than their victories in the War of Independence, had placed Israel on the world map, brought out clearly the unique nature of her position in the Middle East, and drawn the attention of the nations to her security problems. Understanding of Israel's unique situation and the discrimination shown by the United Nations against the young State at last began to dawn, not only in the United States of America but also in Europe, Asia, and Africa. A characteristic indication of this tendency was a statement by M. Paul-Henri Spaak—first President of the U.N. Assembly and formerly Secretary of the North Atlantic Treaty Organization, who is now Foreign Minister of Belgium—which was published in *Foreign Affairs,* the important American quarterly. In an article on the United Nations, M. Spaak wrote:

In the present United Nations setup, which is not what its founders wished and hoped it would be, everything short of war is allowed. Treaties may be violated, promises can be broken, a nation is licensed to menace its neighbor or to perpetrate any sort of trick on it, just as long as there is no actual war. The attitude of Egypt during the last few months is a case in point.

While Egypt denied transit through the Suez Canal to Israeli ships, sent death commandos onto Israeli soil, violated the Treaty of Constantinople, sent arms to be used against French in Algeria and made preparations to attack its neighbor, the United Nations was powerless to intervene. Such intervention would not come within the scope of the Charter as at present interpreted. But let Israel in desperation send troops into the Sinai Peninsula . . . and they are sure to be condemned. Meanwhile, those who were looking on impassively at the brutal repression of the revolt in Hungary could not find words harsh enough to damn them.

This brand of justice, I repeat, is nothing but a caricature. Such an interpretation of principles amounts to rewarding any nation which is audacious enough to accomplish the most reprehensible act but which very cleverly stops short, not of violence, but of open war.

Mr. Spaak's words were only one indication of the growing awareness by world public opinion of the justness of Israel's resistance to Egypt's violation of international law, the principles of the United Nations, and her own obligations to Israel under the Armistice Agreement.

The political struggle, which began even before the end of the Sinai Campaign, lasted four months, from the beginning of November, 1956, until the beginning of March, 1957, and it consisted of three stages. During the first stage, which continued until February 11, we were opposed by almost the entire world, without any substantial change in attitude. The U.N. Secretary-General adopted an obdurate attitude against Israel such as he had not shown toward any of the Arab states when they refused to submit to the Assembly's decisions or even to comply with the verdict of the Security Council. He stubbornly refused to discuss Israel's demands, even those that had been recognized at the U.N. Assembly, until Israel's forces should withdraw behind the Armistice lines.

The young and small State of Israel thus found itself involved in a grave dispute with two factors of world importance, for which Israel has no less regard than any other country, namely, the United Nations and the

United States of America. The source of the dispute lay in some far-reaching moral questions in international relations: Should the United Nations Organization, with the support of the United States, show discrimination— having one attitude to dictatorial Egypt and another to democratic Israel? Should our enemies be allowed to dispatch to Israel murderers and saboteurs, while Israel was not to be allowed to defend herself? Was the United Nations Organization, with the assistance of the United States, to penalize us because we would not agree to the dual morality of the Egyptian dictator, who insisted on others' complying with all obligations that were to his advantage, while ignoring any bilateral agreement or international obligation that was to the advantage of the other party? Would the United Nations and the United States give the stamp of their approval to a regime of blatant and deliberate discrimination in international relations?

For us, this was a period of acute strain, with emergency Cabinet meeting after emergency Cabinet meeting, and a stream of alarming reports coming in from our embassies abroad. What was happening, of course, was simply another Cold War conflict in which both sides were playing desperately for paramount influence in the Arab Middle East. Once again, it began to look as if Israel would be required to foot the bill. There was, however, the difference that the United States was unwilling to buy Arab good will at heavy cost to its relations with Israel, provided we fulfilled the obligations we had taken on in connection with the United Nations resolutions, and in response to the communications received from President Eisenhower. The Soviet Union, on the other hand, made it clear where its interests lay and did not hesitate to lend to the most obvious Arab distortions of recent history the authority of Marshal Bulganin himself and of the Soviet delegation at the United Nations.

Three weeks after my report to Parliament, I spoke to the officers who had fought in the campaign and heard their stories of the part they and their men had played. For me, the simple narratives were epics of Jewish heroism, and I could not possibly add to them. I was no battalion commander; I had been posted on a different kind of front, one not sown with explosive mines but laid with the traps of intrigues of power politics and world interests in conflict.

Victory, I told those officers, did not always enlarge the victor's might. Britain had won the First and the Second World Wars, and in the second had attested magnificently to her greatness and courage. Yet she had lost the rank of a first world power which she had held without challenge in the nineteenth century; after two decisive victories she had become a second-class power. Germany, vanquished in both wars, had recovered quickly. True, she had been divided in two, but Western Germany was once more strong and solvent. So, wars were not always decisive, nor did victories invariably guarantee fulfilment of the victors' purpose.

We ourselves, it was necessary to remember, were living in two contexts. The first was in the Middle East, where, if we could not hold our own against all comers, we were liable to be blotted out. The other was in the world. There was only one world today, interdependent although disunited, perhaps more quarrelsome than it had ever been, but no longer made up of separate entities. In ancient days, one part knew nothing of the next. China thought itself the entire earth. The Biblical countries were a world of their own. The Roman Empire believed as China did. Now, anything that happened in

155

Jerusalem or Rafah was flashed all over the one world within five minutes, and all nations shared the news, for good or ill, in joy or dread. If the Middle East were insulated as once it had been, for example, during the First Temple period, we might live securely for many years to come, especially after the setback just inflicted on Egypt. But the Middle East was part of the one world, and its affairs were not independent of that world. When our War of Independence was fought, only five independent Arab states belonged to the United Nations. Now there were eleven, with eleven votes against our solitary one. They represented seventy million people; our lone voice spoke for less than two million.

There had been a more important change. Hundreds of millions of people, of nations formerly subservient to colonial powers, had won their freedom and were becoming more and more a factor in world affairs. For centuries, they had been ruled and exploited by white men of the European nations. Although we had lived in Asia centuries before some of the peoples who now occupied that continent and long before others first walked onto the stage of history, and although our past covered four thousand years, we nonetheless belonged to the white race. We were regarded as Europeans, of that same race of white oppressors, although we suffered at the hands of white peoples perhaps more than African former colonies.

There was a third change. Russia had voted in the Assembly with the United States and thirty-one other countries for the establishment of a Jewish State. During the War of Independence, although giving us no direct aid, she did not prevent the other countries of her bloc from helping us. The arms we then had came mostly from Czechoslovakia. As time went on, however, the Soviet

Union returned to her traditional opposition to Jewish revival and Zionism, dating back to Lenin. This tremendous power now supported the Arabs and provided them with armaments, although it could scarcely be ignorant of the Arab rulers' plotting against us.

There was yet another thing. We had just witnessed the crisis in Hungary, where the United Nations had exposed its impotence in the affairs of a country controlled by the Soviet Union. There were only two dominant nations in the world, although in a number of years they might be joined by China and India. The United Nations was helpless in any situation in which these two dominant powers were in conflict, but it could be remarkably energetic in enforcing its decisions when these same powers were in agreement. With Hungary, we had seen how weak the United Nations could be, and the conscience of the free world had been profoundly stirred. The United Nations decided then, as it subsequently did in our case, to demand the evacuation of foreign military forces from Hungary and to send a United Nations representative and observers there, but the decisions, vetoed by the Russians, could not be carried out.

In our case, what happened was the opposite of what had taken place nine years earlier; the resolution against us was supported by the two Great Powers. In such circumstances, it was very difficult for Israel to press its case with the United Nations.

In these nine years, the fear of a new world war had grown beyond measure, for never before had man possessed such weapons of destruction. A global conflict might mean the end of humanity. Colleagues returning from the Asian Socialist Conference held in Bombay at the time of the Sinai Campaign reported that all the delegates—from India, Burma, Ceylon, Indonesia, Japan,

157

and Pakistan (there were no Arab delegates)—had been panic-stricken at the thought that we were on the brink of a third world war. Only on the morning of November 9, when they heard about my broadcast of the previous evening (containing my reply to President Eisenhower and noting our intention to withdraw from Sinai), did they breathe freely again.

Everyone, it seemed, felt that our action had saved the world from a third conflagration. I would not go so far as that, but the story illustrated the dominant feelings of contemporary civilization under the threat of the hydrogen bomb. The same terror motivated the Emergency Session of the Assembly of the United Nations at the beginning of November and, in part, explained its decisions.

For the struggle yet to come, delay meant much to us. We needed it so that the issues might be judged more calmly after the fright and the hysteria had subsided. Of course, there were opponents who would not change their minds no matter what we said or however cogently we pleaded the justice of our cause. I was sure that my letters to Bulganin had not changed his attitude; he already knew what Nasser was, what Kuwatli of Syria was, and the King of Saudi Arabia, and Hussein of Jordan, and still he had his own reasons for supporting them.

But there were other countries in the world, free countries where things could be explained to the people even against the official view, and it was of great importance to us to hold up our withdrawal and gain a respite in which to do that explaining. I did not think that the decisions of the Assembly would be withdrawn or modified, but I believed that we might not be made to carry them out as they stood.

We needed time to make clear to the world that, although the Israel Defense Forces did not have to stay in

158

Sinai, for it never was our intention to conquer one more desert, the Egyptian army should not be there either. The only purpose it could have in Sinai was to menace our peace and survival, and world peace as well. Egypt's obstruction of shipping in the Red Sea could not be countenanced again. Nasser, or whoever took his place, could bar the Suez Canal a second time, and the world needed an alternative route. Navigation through the Straits and the port of Eilat offered that alternative.

We had to make this idea plain to the world. The longer the time at our disposal, the longer the time we were in effective control of the western shore of the Straits, and the greater the number of ships that sailed through the Red Sea and the planes that flew over it, the better our chances for demonstrating to the world the value and importance of the Straits. If we could also lay a pipeline from Eilat to Haifa, or at least to Beersheba, and carry oil from there by rail to Haifa, our case would be strengthened.

In peace or war, oil was essential for every branch of the economy. Through Eilat, it could be brought into the Middle East from east of Suez, without using the Canal. Apart from Egypt, only we had a direct outlet both to the Atlantic through the Mediterranean and to the Indian Ocean through the Red Sea. Only if we succeeded in convincing the nations that this was vital for them as well as for us was there any prospect that we might have free navigation through the Straits.

The struggle ahead might bring us into conflict not only with enemies but also with friends. If there were any people who in the past had shown by deeds their friendship for Israel, it was the American people. How different were the letters from President Eisenhower and Marshal Bulganin demanding our compliance with United Nations decisions and our withdrawal from Sinai! Mr. Eisenhower did not threaten; he used friendly language and, knowing him as I did, I was certain that all he wrote was in earnest.

Still, no one could tell what troubles might be in store for us from America. In the Assembly, the United States and the Soviet Union competed to win over the Afro-Asian bloc. This bloc, under the leadership of India, put its weight behind Nasser. In the eyes of either of the two big powers, any recognition of our just rights and demands would interfere with their attempts to win the confidence of the Afro-Asians. In regard to those nations who were our friends, we would have to enter this struggle with understanding and tolerance.

I could not promise our people that we would be successful. But of one thing I had no doubt at all: Operation Sinai had not been in vain. It was a splendid achievement, and not only from a military point of view. It had changed our status in the world. We were a negligible force no longer. This knowledge, I know, intensified the hostility of our enemies. However, Israel was no longer the same, in its own eyes or the world's, and this was an important gain. The people as a whole felt that something of vast significance in its history had transpired. Every Jew would hold his head higher; every Jew, wherever he was, was proud of the Israeli army and the State.

Despite the attack on us in the United Nations, at the outset reinforced by Bulganin and Eisenhower, with the Eastern, Asian, and African blocs, and some European countries in support, anyone who believed that the effects of the Sinai Campaign had been nullified was badly mistaken. The struggle, nevertheless, would be difficult and long. All we could do was to explain the merits of our case. Survival and security depended on our strength; now we would have to prove our rights to the world.

Chapter Ten
Israel Withdraws

By stages, we set about withdrawing our forces from the Sinai Peninsula in accordance with the resolutions of the United Nations General Assembly. But Sharm el-Sheikh, at the tip of the peninsula, our only guarantee of freedom of navigation through the Straits of Tiran, was still a cause of dispute between Israel and the United Nations. The destiny of the Gaza Strip and the issue of Egyptian belligerency were still unresolved. And it was now the end of January, 1957; no dependable settlement in the Middle East was anywhere in sight.

However, an understanding of Israel's security problems had begun to show itself. One indication of this change was the above-mentioned statement by Mr. Paul-Henri Spaak, who had presided over the first meeting of the General Assembly called to deal with the Sinai problem.

In my letter of November 8, 1956, to President Eisenhower, I had written that we were ready to withdraw from the Sinai area "when satisfactory arrangements are made with the United Nations Emergency Force." We had conveyed the same information to the Secretary-General, and in a letter to him on November 21 we defined "satisfactory arrangements" as those that would safeguard Israel against acts of hostility on land and at sea.

The Assembly's resolution of November 4 stated that the task of the Emergency Force was "to secure and supervise the cessation of hostilities." We were entitled to expect that the force would not allow the Sinai Desert to again become a base for aggression against Israel. Despite misgivings, we did not suspend our withdrawal, and by the end of January we had evacuated the whole 20,000-odd square miles of the desert except for the narrow strip of the coast at Sharm el-Sheikh. That was our guarantee of freedom of navigation in the Gulf of Aqaba for all vessels, including Arab ships. We had no wish to remain at Sharm el-Sheikh, and it was our intention to evacuate as soon as we received dependable assurances that there would be no interference there with the freedom of Israeli or international shipping in the Straits of Tiran.

The principle of free navigation in all seas and straits, one sanctified in international law, is accepted unreservedly in the family of nations. It is no less important than the universal doctrine that it is wrong to occupy the territory of another state. Both in the Straits of Tiran and in the Suez Canal, the principle of free navigation had been violated by Egypt for years, and Egypt now publicly proclaimed that she would go on violating it. To give up Sharm el-Sheikh without the guarantees on which we insisted would, therefore, have meant that we ourselves were abetting Egypt's violation of international law.

162

The coast there, like the greater part of Sinai, is a bleak, waterless, uninhabited desert. Until the boycott and blockade were organized by the Arab League, there was no Egyptian force in the bay. Then troops were sent in by Egypt to deny our approach by sea to Eilat. Year after year this illegal action continued. The United Nations, unconcerned about the fate of shipping so essential to Israel and far from negligible in international trade, did nothing to stop it.

The Gaza Strip posed a unique problem. We felt that no United Nations force would be able to prevent the reorganization of the *fedayun* by the Egyptian authorities in that area, or to prevent their being sent once again into Israeli territory. With due regard for the stand taken by the General Assembly, we ourselves had no intention of maintaining armed forces in the Strip. What we felt to be desirable was that our civil services should remain in the Strip until an effective relationship had been established between us and the United Nations. Our administration was in a position to safeguard internal security, to continue the development of self-government in the towns and villages, and to insure progress in such public services as health, education, electricity supply, irrigation, communications, agriculture, trade, and industry. We were willing to do all we could to alleviate the wretched conditions of the 60,000 impoverished permanent residents of the Gaza Strip and to help secure reasonable conditions and a decent standard of living for them.

We were well aware of the problem of the refugees in the Gaza Strip, a part of the general problem of the Arab refugees. There was no sphere in which the moral failure of the Arab states had been so palpably demonstrated. A small and poor country, Israel had managed

163

to absorb hundreds of thousands of refugees, a great many of them Jews in flight from Arab countries. Yet those very countries, most of them spacious and sparsely populated, would under no circumstances settle the Arab refugees, preferring to exploit them as a political weapon against Israel. Together, the United Nations, Israel, and the refugees could make a serious bid at solving the problems of the area. If, however, Egypt's influence was restored in the Strip, either by the return of her army or in some indirect way with the entry of the Emergency Force, all constructive prospects for the area would be frustrated and it would revert to lawlessness and misfortune.

Having evacuated the whole of the Sinai Desert, except for the strip of coast on the Straits, we felt it our right and our duty to appeal to the United Nations to prevent the area from again becoming a base of aggression. Apart from El Arish, Tur, and the Monastery of St. Catherine, which were non-Egyptian centers, there was no center of population in the Sinai Desert. Even after the area was taken from the Ottoman Empire by the British and handed over to Egypt, the latter never regarded it as a place for settlement; Egypt had not accomplished there in decades what Israel had done in a few years in the Negev. Egypt had not even attempted to settle a single Arab refugee in the few oases of Sinai. We appealed to the United Nations to demilitarize this area to prevent future disputes between Israel and Egypt. Our stand was dictated by our conscience, our right to live, our sense of justice, and our fervent hope for a genuine peace in the Middle East.

On February 2, 1957, the United Nations Assembly again adopted two resolutions. The first expressed displeasure at Israel's failure to complete her withdrawal behind the Armistice lines and required her to do so without further delay. In the second resolution, the Assembly recognized, *inter alia,* that Israel's withdrawal must be followed by action to insure progress toward the establishment of peaceful conditions.

In the dispute between the Government of Israel and the United States, every effort was made not to close the door to further talks. On February 3, I received a letter from President Eisenhower, friendly but administering a grave warning: the resolutions had been submitted with a view to bringing about peaceful conditions, but the first step must be the completion of Israel's withdrawal.

In reply to his letter, I wrote on February 8:

Dear Mr. President,

I thank you for your message dated February 3. I am sincerely grateful for your personal interest and fully share the wish for the continuance and deepening of the friendly relations between the United States and Israel. The Government of Israel is at one with you in deep concern for the establishment of peace and tranquillity in the Middle East. In response to your appeal of November 7, we started the evacuation of our troops from the Sinai Desert, although it was the overwhelming sentiment of our people that effective assurances for our security must first be obtained. We continued our withdrawal despite the fact that Egypt refused to abandon its state of war against us. Our troops have evacuated Sinai—an area of more than 50,000 square kilometers—except for a narrow strip on the west coast of the Gulf of Aqaba which ensures freedom of navigation in the Gulf. We have informed the United Nations that we have no intention to hold this

165

strip and will evacuate it as soon as effective assurances will be forthcoming for continued freedom of passage.

I have to record with regret that in this matter the United Nations has applied different standards to Egypt and to Israel. For eight years Egypt acted in disregard of the Armistice Agreement and of the Charter and pursued a policy of belligerency towards Israel. It defied an express resolution of the Security Council in denying us free transit through the Suez Canal and broke its pledged word in regard to the freedom of shipping in the Gulf of Aqaba. I refer to a solemn undertaking made by Egypt through the American Ambassador in Cairo on January 28, 1950. This policy took a heavy toll of Israeli lives and caused us severe economic damage. It was part of an overall plan to eliminate Israel by force. Those who have the power and the authority to intervene took no effective steps whatever to end these flagrant violations of international obligations. . . .

We are prepared to withdraw our forces forthwith from Sharm el-Sheikh if continued freedom of passage through the Straits is assured. We are equally ready to evacuate our military forces from the Gaza Strip without delay and to leave there only a civil administration and police, in suitable relationship with the United Nations. Such arrangements alone would ensure peace and stability in the area, would give to the local population a real share in the administration, would set them on the path to economic self-sufficiency, and would offer the hope of working out a better future for the refugees in an atmosphere free from Egyptian incitement.

Under the Charter of the United Nations are we not

like other states entitled to security from attack? With deepest respect I would ask you, Mr. President, why no effective action was taken by the Government of the United States and by the other governments which supported the proposals of the United States in the General Assembly, to give us such security. . . .

In your letter you referred to the possibility of United Nations "procedures" being invoked against Israel for not having carried out in full the resolutions of the General Assembly. No such "procedures" were ever invoked against Egypt, which for years past has violated resolutions of the Security Council and provisions of the Charter and continues so to do. At a time when public opinion in most of the free countries of the world has come to acknowledge the justice of our stand, is it conceivable that the United States, the land of freedom, equality, and human rights, should support such discrimination and that United Nations "procedures" should be invoked to force us back into a position which would again expose us to murder and blockade?

Mr. President, in the Law which we received more than 3,000 years ago on Mount Sinai and which has become part of mankind's heritage, the message went forth that there shall be no discrimination between man and man and between nation and nation. Throughout millennia of persecution our people have not lost faith in ultimate justice, peace, and human equality. It is unthinkable that now that we have recovered our independence in our ancient homeland we should submit to discrimination. Our people will never accept this no matter what sacrifice it may entail. Israel though small is entitled to security, freedom, and equal rights in the family of nations. Like any other independent nation, Israel is free as of right, and our people are determined to defend their independence.

The question is not a legalistic one. It affects the very foundations of international morality: will the United Nations apply one measure to Egypt and another to Israel? . . .

More than any man now living, you, Mr. President, may be able to help in putting an end to all this hostility and establishing peace between our neighbors and ourselves.

Permit me in conclusion to thank you for your kind interest in my well-being, which I deeply appreciate.

Sincerely yours,
DAVID BEN-GURION

The tremendous effort of our embassy in Washington and our delegation to the United Nations left their mark on American public opinion. The press and Congressional circles showed considerable understanding of Israel's attitude and the justice of her cause, and the pressure of public opinion led to a change in United States policy which marked the beginning of what I called the second stage of our struggle.

On February 11, the American Secretary of State, John Foster Dulles, published, with the approval of President Eisenhower, an *aide-mémoire* that had been handed to the Israeli Ambassador in Washington. The following are the salient points of the document:

The United Nations General Assembly has sought specifically, vigorously, and almost unanimously, the prompt withdrawal from Egypt of the armed forces of Britain, France, and Israel. Britain and France have complied unconditionally. The forces of Israel have

168

been withdrawn to a considerable extent but still hold Egyptian territory at Sharm el-Sheikh at the entrance to the Gulf of Aqaba. They also occupy the Gaza Strip, which is territory specified by the armistice arrangement to be occupied by Egypt. . . .

We recognize that the area has been a source of armed infiltration and reprisal back and forth contrary to the Armistice Agreement, and is a source of great potential danger because of the presence there of so large a number of Arab refugees—about 200,000. Accordingly, we believe that the United Nations General Assembly and the Secretary-General should seek that the United Nations Emergency Force, in the exercise of its mission, move into this area and be on the boundary between Israel and the Gaza Strip. . . .

With respect to the Gulf of Aqaba and access thereto —the United States believes that the Gulf comprehends international waters and that no nation has the right to prevent free and innocent passage in the Gulf and through the Straits giving access thereto. We have in mind not only commercial usage, but the passage of pilgrims on religious missions, which should be fully respected.

The United States recalls that on January 28, 1950, the Egyptian Ministry of Foreign Affairs informed the United States that the Egyptian occupation of the two islands of Tiran and Sanafir at the entrance of the Gulf of Aqaba was only to protect the islands themselves against possible damage or violation and that "this occupation being in no way conceived in a spirit of obstructing in any way innocent passage through the stretch of water separating these two islands from the Egyptian coast of Sinai, it follows that this passage, the only practicable one, will remain free as in the past, in conformity with international practice and recognized principles of the law of nations."

In the absence of some overriding decision to the contrary, as by the International Court of Justice, the United States, on behalf of vessels of United States registry, is prepared to exercise the right of free and innocent passage and to join with others to secure general recognition of this right.

It is of course clear that the enjoyment of a right of free and innocent passage by Israel would depend upon its prior withdrawal in accordance with the United Nations resolutions. The United States has no reason to assume that any littoral state would under these circumstances obstruct the right of free and innocent passage.

The United States is prepared publicly to declare that it will use its influence in concert with other United Nations members, to the end that, following Israel's withdrawal, these other measures [the United Nations decision of February 2 that the United Nations Emergency Force "move into the Straits area as the Israeli forces are withdrawn"] will be implemented.

We believe that our views and purposes in this respect are shared by many other nations and that a tranquil future for Israel is best assured by reliance upon that fact, rather than by an occupation in defiance of the overwhelming judgment of the world community.

The Government of Israel gave very serious consideration to this document and conducted talks with Secretary of State Dulles to clarify a number of points. In our memorandum, we expressed appreciation of the efforts of the President and the Secretary of State to seek a solution to

170

the two problems of the Straits of Tiran and the Gaza Strip. We welcomed the positive approach of the United States to the question of free navigation through the Straits of Tiran and the Gulf of Aqaba, and the Secretary of State's pertinent reference to the Egyptian undertaking of 1950 in regard to the Straits.

We welcomed, also, the statement that the United Nations Emergency Force should move into Sharm el-Sheikh, but noted that recognition of the free right of passage through the Gulf did not in itself guarantee that right for Israel, as had been shown in the matter of the Suez Canal. We therefore considered it to be imperative that the Emergency Force should remain in the area until a peace settlement or some other effective and reliable arrangement had been reached.

On the subject of the Gaza Strip, we pointed out that all we wanted there was concrete assurance that Egypt would not be reinstated in the area that she had converted into a base of aggression against us. While we welcomed Secretary Dulles' *aide-mémoire*, we could not, therefore, regard it as satisfactory, since it required our withdrawal behind the Armistice line in the Gaza Strip and our evacuation of the shores of the Straits of Tiran in advance of a settlement of either one of these problems.

While these exchanges were going on, the sitting of the Assembly of the United Nations had been suspended, but the demand of the Arab and Soviet blocs for the imposition of sanctions had grown more insistent.

On February 18, I sent an urgent appeal to Mr. Dulles, asking for the adjournment of the Assembly's deliberations for a short time, so that an impartial committee could come to Israel—and if need be, to Egypt—for the purpose of seeking an agreed settlement on the questions associated with Sharm el-Sheikh and the Gaza Strip. I

171

emphasized that if the United Nations, with American support, compelled Israel to withdraw by threatening the imposition of sanctions, the moral basis of the Organization would be undermined. I felt that there were grounds for expecting that a thorough investigation on the spot by United Nations representatives could lead to a settlement.

I had no reply from Secretary Dulles to this appeal, but two days later a message arrived from President Eisenhower saying that, in response to my appeal, the United States delegation had supported the proposal to postpone the deliberations of the General Assembly. An adjournment, however, was out of the question, and in the absence of an affirmative decision from Israel, there was no certainty that the renewed deliberations would not involve grave consequences. It was the President's hope that we would immediately announce our compliance with the demand for withdrawal and rely on the determination of all friends of justice to bring about a state of affairs that would conform to the principles of justice and international law and serve impartially the proper interests of all in the area. He added that, after consultations with Congressional leaders, he intended to broadcast on these questions to the American people.

On the same day, President Eisenhower made his broadcast, which contained the following points:

1. The United States had no ambitions or desires in the Middle East, other than that each country there might maintain its independence and live peacefully within itself and with its neighbors.

2. The United States realized that military action against Egypt resulted from grave and repeated provocations. But it believed that the use of military force

to solve international disputes could not be reconciled with the principles and purposes of the United Nations.

3. Israeli forces had been withdrawn from much of the territory of Egypt which they had occupied, but Israeli forces still remained outside the Armistice lines, and they [the Government of the United States] were approaching a fateful moment when either they must recognize that the United Nations was unable to restore peace in the area or the United Nations must renew with increased vigor its efforts to bring about Israel's withdrawal.

4. If Israel withdrew, the United Nations should see that in the Middle East there would be a greater degree of justice and compliance with international law than had been the case prior to the events of October-November, 1956.

5. The United States had been a co-sponsor of the United Nations resolution and had thus sought to assure that Israel would, for the future, enjoy her rights under the Armistice and under international law.

6. Neither the United States nor the United Nations had authority to impose upon the parties a substantial modification of the Armistice Agreement, which was freely signed by Israel and Egypt.

7. Nevertheless, the United States, as a member of the United Nations, would seek such disposition of the United Nations Emergency Force as would assure that the Gaza Strip could no longer be a source of armed infiltration and reprisals.

8. The United States would urge and support some participation by the United Nations, with the approval of Egypt, in the administration of the Gaza Strip.

9. With reference to the Gulf of Aqaba, the United States expressed the conviction that the Gulf consti-

173

tuted international waters and that no nation had the right to prevent free and innocent passage in the Gulf. The United Nations Emergency Force should remain in Egyptian territory to assure the avoidance of belligerent acts.

10. Peace and justice were two sides of the same coin, and perhaps the world community had been at fault in not having paid enough attention to this truth. The United Nations would vigorously seek solutions of the problem of the area in accordance with justice and international law.

11. The United Nations should exert pressure upon Israel to comply with the withdrawal resolution.

12. Egypt, by accepting the six principles adopted by the Security Council in relation to the Suez Canal on October 13, 1956, bound herself to free and open transit through the Canal without discrimination.

13. It should not be assumed that if Israel withdrew, Egypt would prevent Israeli shipping from using the Suez Canal or the Gulf of Aqaba. If, unhappily, Egypt thereafter violated the Armistice Agreements or other international obligations, this should be firmly dealt with by the society of nations.

That same evening, I informed President Eisenhower that I had no right to decide on my own responsibility, but I would submit his message to the Government the next day and inform him accordingly. The next day I informed him that our Ambassador, Mr. Eban, was returning to Washington with instructions, and it was our hope that we might reach a mutual understanding.

Mr. Eban was instructed to endeavor to separate the settlement on free passage in the Gulf of Aqaba from the problem of the Gaza Strip, and to make an effort to arrive

at a settlement on free passage. He was to inform the
United States and other member states that, consistently
with the attitude we had taken all along, we would withdraw from the Straits if our freedom of passage was assured (1) by the presence of an Emergency Force, (2)
by guarantees from various countries, (3) by an agreement between the four littoral states, or (4) by any other
arrangement satisfactory to us. As for the Strip, we suggested a United Nations committee to discuss its future,
but we would not countenance the return of Egypt.

It was quickly made clear to us in New York and in
Washington that the two problems could not be separated, and we were again faced with a complete dead-
lock. The United Nations Assembly and the Government
of the United States refused to budge from their position
that a prior condition for the safeguarding of freedom of
passage was the withdrawal of Israel's forces from Sharm
el-Sheikh and the Gaza Strip.

Two resolutions were submitted in the Assembly. One,
by the Arab states, demanded economic, political, and
military sanctions against Israel. The second, by the
United States, contained an ultimatum to Israel to withdraw her forces within three to five days, with measures
to be taken against her if she did not comply within that
period.

In the meantime, the Assembly was postponed for a
few days, on a proposal from the United States, so that
talks could be held with Israel. It was at this crucial point,
in the last days of February, that Canada and France
took a hand in the negotiations, and thus opened the third
and final stage of the struggle.

We had come to a turning point. However, an element
of hopefulness and reassurance had been injected into
the conflict by the representatives of France and Can-

ada. They proposed that Israel's right should be safe-guarded not *by* the United Nations, for that could not now be brought about, but *within* the United Nations. This meant that a number of influential nations, especially the maritime states, would make two declarations at the Assembly, affirming (1) the freedom of passage in the Straits of Tiran, Israel's right to freedom of shipping, and their own intention to send their ships to Eilat, and (2) Israel's right to self-defense under the terms of Article 51 of the United Nations Charter, which would be invoked if there was interference by force with Israel's shipping in the Straits.

A similar declaration would be made about the Gaza Strip: that the United Nations Emergency Force would remain there until peace was assured.

These two friendly countries brought no pressure to bear on Israel to accept their view. We were free to heed their advice or reject it. It was clear, however, that this was the last and most practical opportunity for the settlement of the two problems, and we would have the support of friendly world opinion. In the existing situation, it was the only way we could have Israeli and international shipping in the Gulf of Aqaba and the Red Sea.

We had always maintained that we had no interest in Sharm el-Sheikh except to safeguard navigation, and now we had seen demonstrated the growing conviction among the nations that the Gulf was an international waterway. Mr. Dulles's *aide-mémoire* of February 11 had made it plain that the United States was also ready to make use of freedom of passage in the Gulf and would co-operate with other countries to assure its universal recognition. The *aide-mémoire* affirmed that, in accordance with the Asembly's second resolution of February 2, the Emergency Force would occupy Sharm el-Sheikh after the Israeli withdrawal, and that it was universally recognized that its functions in the Straits included prevention of acts of hostility.

Moreover, the United States delegate to the Assembly, on both January 28 and February 2, had declared that it was the duty of the Emergency Force in the Straits to keep the land and sea forces of Israel and Egypt apart until it became clear that no belligerent acts were being performed, and that the peaceful conditions requisite in a waterway of international importance obtained in fact.

We still viewed with concern the possibility that the Emergency Force might be precipitately withdrawn, passage again obstructed, and hostilities renewed. A premature withdrawal of the Emergency Force could do grave harm to international interests and jeopardize regional peace and security. We therefore sought and secured an undertaking, contained in a memorandum from the Secretary-General on February 26, that any proposal to withdraw the Emergency Force from the Straits must first be submitted to the Advisory Committee which represented the General Assembly in the implementation of the decision of November 2, 1956. This procedure would enable the United Nations to insure that no hasty step was taken which might provoke hostilities.

We also had reason to believe that many members of the United Nations would be guided by the policy expressed by the United States delegate on February 2: to maintain the Emergency Force in the Straits until peaceful conditions were established there.

In the light of these principles and policies which had been expressed and laid down, and in light of the arrangements of the United Nations and the maritime countries, on March 1, on the authority of the Government of

177

Israel, the Israeli Minister for Foreign Affairs announced in the Assembly that Israel would evacuate the Gaza Strip and Sharm el-Sheikh.

Our Minister also announced that Israel was withdrawing from the Gaza Strip on the following assumptions: (1) that the take-over from the military and civilian control of Israel would be exclusively by the United Nations Emergency Force; (2) that the force would carry out functions enumerated by the Secretary-General, namely: to safeguard life and property in the area by providing effective and efficient police protection, to guarantee good civilian administration, to assure maximum assistance to United Nations plans for dealing with the refugee problem, and to foster the economic development of the territory and its people; and (3) that the responsibility of the United Nations in the administration of the Strip would be maintained until there was a peace settlement, to be sought as rapidly as possible, or a definite agreement on the future of the Strip.

Our Minister also announced that it was Israel's understanding that freedom of passage would be insured in the Straits of Tiran and that the United Nations Emergency Force would remain at Sharm el-Sheikh and would carry out the functions mentioned in the Secretary-General's memorandum. Israel would reserve the right to defend freedom of passage by force. If conditions arose in the Gaza Strip indicating a repetition of disturbances, Israel would reserve her freedom to act in defense of her rights.

On the days immediately following the declaration of our Foreign Minister, statements were made by the delegates of the United States, France, Costa Rica, Argentina, Panama, Holland, Norway, Belgium, Australia, New Zealand, Sweden, Canada, Portugal, Italy, Denmark, and others. All these declarations added weight to the Foreign

Minister's statement, but several points in the statement by Henry Cabot Lodge, the United States representative, aroused grave concern among us and our friends.

Mr. Lodge recalled President Eisenhower's broadcast of February 20 and the two resolutions of February 2. The United States, he said, had taken note of our declaration, which constituted restatements of what had already been said by the Assembly or by the Secretary-General, or hopes and expectations which, he said, seemed not unreasonable. The withdrawal, in his view, was not conditional. The United States believed that the future of the Gaza Strip must, from a juridical standpoint, be worked out within the framework of the Armistice Agreement and hoped that the United Nations administration would remain in the Strip until a final settlement between the parties was reached.

As for the Gulf, he repeated his statements of January 28 and February 2. In his Government's view, the Gulf of Aqaba was an international waterway, and no nation had the right to interfere with free and innocent passage in it and in the Straits leading to it. The United States was prepared to exercise the right of free and innocent passage and to join with others to secure general recognition of that right. The Emergency Force on the Straits should stay there according to the recommendations of the Secretary-General's Advisory Committee, which would judge whether the matter should be presented to the Assembly.

The American delegate's allusion to the working out of the future of the Gaza Strip "within the framework of the Armistice Agreement" aroused concern not only in the Israeli delegation but among our friends in the United Nations as well. We did not conceal this concern from the American Government, and our withdrawal was held up until the following letter from President Eisenhower to me was published on March 2:

My dear Mr. Prime Minister,

I was indeed deeply gratified at the decision of your Government to withdraw promptly and fully behind the Armistice lines as set out by your Foreign Minister in her address of yesterday to the General Assembly. I venture to express the hope that the carrying out of these withdrawals will go forward with the utmost speed.

I know that this decision was not an easy one. I believe, however, that Israel will have no cause to regret having thus conformed to the strong sentiment of the world community as expressed in the various United Nations resolutions relating to withdrawal.

It has always been the view of this Government that after the withdrawal there should be a united effort by all of the nations to bring about conditions in the area more stable, more tranquil, and more conducive to the general welfare than those which existed heretofore. Already the United Nations General Assembly has adopted resolutions which presage such a better future. Hopes and expectations based thereon were voiced by your Foreign Minister and others. I believe that it is reasonable to entertain such hopes and expectations and I want you to know that the United States, as a friend of all of the countries of the area and as a loyal member of the United Nations, will seek that such hopes prove not to be vain.

I am, my dear Mr. Prime Minister,

Sincerely,

DWIGHT D. EISENHOWER

Chapter Eleven
Looking to the Future

Both in the Cabinet and in Parliament, there were those who opposed our evacuation of the Gaza Strip and the coast of the Straits. If some of my colleagues believed it was a mistake, the responsibility rested with me, for I, fully aware of all the dangerous prospects involved, advised the Government to accept the proposal. I am prepared, in perfect peace of mind, to accept the burden of this "mistake" before history and the Jewish people, but perhaps I should explain my own reasons for supporting the decision to withdraw, since not all my colleagues shared them.

Of all the dangerous prospects, the one most likely to materialize was the return of the Egyptians to the Gaza Strip, either as a civilian administration or through military occupation, relying on the pretext of the Armistice Agreement. Our settlements on the borders, in the south, and in the Negev, had heard with deep anxiety of our decision to withdraw, but in my deliberations I had never ignored the fact that the Gaza Strip, under any administration, would remain a source of trouble so long as the refugees were not resettled. Anyone who spoke of the Strip without understanding all the complications and risks arising out of the composition of the population was living in a fool's paradise.

I was convinced all along that the least harmful and least dangerous administration for Gaza would be one jointly exercised by Israel and the United Nations. Until a solution of the refugee problem was found and a peace settlement between Egypt and Israel arrived at, an Israeli administration alone or a United Nations administration alone would involve greater dangers than a joint venture. However, it was not possible to achieve a joint administration, and the composition of the United Nations made it just as unlikely in the future.

As for the Straits, there was no express United Nations decision that the Emergency Force must remain in the Strip until a peace settlement was made. Only the Advisory Committee could decide that the force should not be withdrawn and replaced by Egyptian troops. On the other hand, there was the declaration of all the principal maritime states that the Gulf and the Straits are an international waterway and all nations have the right to free passage. These states had declared that they would exercise this right and would send their ships to Eilat. They had taken note of our declaration that we would be able to defend ourselves by force if our rights were infringed and had expressly recorded their recognition of our rights.

If our forces had remained in Sharm el-Sheikh, we would have been able to defend our right to freedom of shipping; but if we had remained, there would have been no actual shipping, for we would have been generally condemned by all other countries, and no foreign nation would have sent its ships to Eilat. The oil that we meant to send from Eilat to Haifa would not even have reached our southern port. However, our occupation of Sharm el-Sheikh had not been in vain. It had not insured Israeli or international shipping in the Gulf, but it had stirred opinion throughout the world to an appreciation of the maritime importance of the Gulf. The maritime powers were no longer content to be dependent on the Suez Canal, and if they kept their promises, the Gulf could become an international waterway, not only in theory but in fact. Eilat could become a port of first importance.

Even before the foundation of the State, there were those who saw the potentialities of Eilat and the Red Sea and labored to re-establish this first Jewish port in history. During the War of Independence, it was impossible to get to Eilat, for it is situated at the tip of a triangle whose two sides are enemy territory—Jordan on one side, Egypt on the other. It was a deathtrap for any Jewish force, although it had been assigned to Israel by the United Nations resolution of November 27, 1947. Only after we had concluded an Armistice Agreement with Egypt, which confirmed the assignment of Eilat to Israel, could our troops be sent to take possession of the Bay and Israel's flag be raised beside the Red Sea.

Eilat was only a name then; when we withdrew from the Straits it was already a township of about 1,200. Today, it has about 7,000 inhabitants. We aimed to create a port of international importance, like Haifa, one which would be a gateway for us to the peoples of Asia and Africa. There was much hope for economic ties with them, and cultural ties as well.

What we hoped to achieve in Eilat could not be accomplished in a day. We needed a vigorous, constructive

183

effort to build a deepwater port, to develop efficient, modern land transportation between Eilat and the Mediterranean, to lay an oil pipeline, to build a chain of settlements along the road from Eilat to Beersheba, and to insure a plentiful supply of water for the expanding port town. It would call for a large investment of capital and the powerful impetus of pioneers. But all this meant clear and safe access to Eilat from the Red Sea. It meant freedom of passage in the Straits of Tiran.

We did not wage war to seize Sinai or to force peace on Nasser, and after the Sinai Campaign I had no hopes for an early peace. Nasser was in no hurry; he could wait. The occupation of Port Said and Suez had probably bothered him more than the occupation of Sinai, and I believe that even if we had remained in Sinai for as long as five years, Nasser would still have bided his time and not made peace. He did not want peace. He could have feared that if he were reconciled with Israel, somebody else in the Egyptian army would arise and depose him. Was it conceivable that he would make peace with us so that the authorities in Baghdad could charge him with treason to the Arabs? No one who understood the harsh realities of Arab politics could have expected peace from Nasser at that time.

There was another reason, a very serious one, for my support of our withdrawal. During the four months that our forces had been in Gaza and on the coast of the Straits, we had been successful in explaining our case and securing the support of public opinion in the free world. The world was at last awake to the danger of the *fedayun* and the problem of our security in the Strip. For eight years, while we suffered murder, sabotage, and theft, the world had looked on unheeding, and the

184

United Nations had remained apathetic. The Sinai Campaign had changed that; the problem of our security had been brought to the attention of the world.

Israel's security had become a question of conscience for many nations, and we were urged to give the family of nations the opportunity to live up to the moral responsibility it had asumed: to spare us a renewal of blockade, boycott, and murderous attacks from the Egyptians and the other Arab countries.

The representatives of many nations had publicly confessed that the United Nations had not fulfilled its obligations toward Israel. It was my conviction that just as we could not submit to external duress, so we could not treat lightly the moral claim addressed to us. Policy cannot be dogmatic or static, and I felt that it would be wrong to ignore the changes in world public opinion and on the international scene.

We had fought, and not unsuccessfully, against the double standard of the United Nations, which implied one law for Israel and another for Egypt. The United States and other nations had made statements which involved a moral commitment. We had to test the true value of these undertakings.

There was a final and decisive consideration. The Israel Defense Forces were still far from the limits of their capacity. They needed to increase their strength, to improve their training and their combat capacity, and to acquire more effective and modern weapons. I am well aware of the importance of high morale in a conflict of arms, but without the right weapons, the bravest and best of soldiers is lost. It is not simple to equip an army, and the best that money could buy a couple of years ago is obsolete today. There was no immediate prospect that the Soviet Union would supply arms to us, but there was not the slightest doubt that it would continue to send arms to Egypt and Syria.

With these considerations in mind I asked myself: What would happen if we refused the proposal of France and Canada, the two nations who had offered us such significant help in the past, and then found ourselves condemned by the United Nations, the United States, and the Soviet Union? What would happen in a year or two if we had to escort our shipping in the Straits of Tiran and the Gulf of Aqaba? Nasser and his allies would once again have a choice and abundant supply of Soviet arms, while all doors would be closed to us. Frankly, I was not prepared to assume this tremendous responsibility for the course of Jewish history. Nor would I advise any successor of mine to do such a thing. General George C. Marshall had described the Sinai Campaign as one of the most brilliant battles in world history, but we could not allow ourselves to be intoxicated by victory. I was not prepared to place Israel in such a position that if she had to defend her shipping or her existence she would find all the friendly markets of the world closed to her.

I knew when I submitted my proposal for withdrawal to the Cabinet on March 1 that I was doing the most unpopular thing, but I knew that it was a vital and necessary act. The border settlers and the defense forces are dearest of all to me. I knew what their feelings would be —the disappointment, the bitterness, and the anxiety— yet I felt it to be my solemn duty.

Perhaps we had fallen short of achieving all we wanted and deserved, but I was grateful for what the Sinai Campaign had given us. Like all Jews everywhere, I was proud of our achievement. Finally, I was proud of the courage shown by our Government in making the decision to withdraw, a decision that was unpopular, but wise, beneficial, and honorable. In my mind, even the decision to withdraw will live in Jewish history as a decisive stage in the progress of the State of Israel toward the consummation of its independence.

Chapter Twelve
Southwards!

Over six years have passed since the Sinai Campaign. Some of my colleagues at home and friends of Israel abroad were sincerely apprehensive that our action would arouse the antagonism of the Asian and African peoples, and during the first few weeks after the campaign there seemed to be grounds for their apprehensions. But the past six years have shown that these fears were not justified. Israel has won the respect and admiration of Asian and African peoples, and the valor of the Israel Defense Forces at Sinai has made no small contribution to this attitude. Never since the War of Independence has there been such a measure of relative tranquillity on the borders. We have won freedom of navigation in the Straits of Eilat and the Red Sea; Israeli and foreign ships bring passengers and freight to and from Eilat. The oil flows from Eilat to Haifa, and with the completion of the first-class highway to Beersheba there is now for the first time in history a good road link, through Israel, from the Red Sea to the Mediterranean, creating what we are justified in calling "Israel's dry-land Suez Canal."

But it would be a dangerous illusion to imagine that the Sinai Campaign has completely solved the problem of our security. It has undoubtedly improved our position considerably. It has enhanced security on the borders and for some time has deterred our neighbors from challenging Israel. Basically, however, the problem has not been solved; it is doubtful whether war can solve historical problems at all, although sometimes it is unavoidable to stave off some great and growing immediate danger, as in the struggle against Hitler on the world scale or the Sinai Campaign in the Middle East. The possibility of peace between Israel and the Arab peoples—and that is the supreme goal of our foreign policy—depends in large measure on our having sufficient military strength to constitute an effective deterrent and on our position in the international arena. Only if the Arab rulers are convinced that Israel cannot be liquidated, either by military measures or by blockade and isolation, will they ultimately realize the need for, and the value of, peace and co-operation with Israel.

Military strength depends, however, not only on the equipment, training, and morale of our armed forces but, first and foremost, on the way we meet our challenges at home. After the Sinai Campaign, more than ever before, we needed to concentrate a growing proportion of our efforts and resources on the still barren southern half of the country. In the south and the Negev stood the cradle of our people; they are Israel's weak points and danger zones; they are also her greatest hope.

When our Father Abraham was commanded to leave his country, his kindred, and his father's house in Ur of

189

the Chaldees, and go to the Promised Land, he journeyed constantly toward the south—in Hebrew, the Negev—and, after hunger compelled him to go to Egypt, he again returned to the same area. For a time he pitched his tent in the plains of Mamre near Hebron, since the arid land in the south could not sustain both Abraham and Lot, for both of them had much substance—sheep and cattle. But after the overthrow of Sodom, Abraham returned "toward the land of the South, and dwelt between Kadesh and Shur, and he sojourned in Gerar" (Genesis 20:1). His neighbors were Philistines who had settled in the southwest, and the Father of the Hebrews made a covenant with them after the quarrels in connection with the well which he dug in that arid land, and he called the place Beersheba—"the Well of the Oath"— "because there they swore both of them" (Genesis 21:31).

Our Book of Books is distinguished for its dramatic conciseness, even when it deals with great events. It mentions in one verse, ten Hebrew words, two actions on the part of Abraham, the collocation of which arouses profound astonishment at the unique insight of our forebears. In one breath the Bible combines an apparently prosaic and everyday act—the planting of a tree—with the brilliant expression of the supreme concept which underlies the original world outlook of Judaism: the concept of a Supreme God. These are the words: "And Abraham planted a tamarisk-tree in Beer-sheba, and called there on the name of the Lord, the Everlasting God" (Genesis 21:33). Only the ancient Jewish genius had the capacity and the boldness to combine in one verse, with such concise simplicity, two such different and profoundly significant acts.

Isaac, Abraham's son, also lived in the land of the Negev, and here he met Rebecca when she came from Aram-Naharaim. He, too, was involved in difficulties with his neighbors in connection with the digging of wells, which the Philistines stopped up.

> And Isaac's servants digged in the valley, and found there a well of living water. And the herdmen of Gerar strove with Isaac's herdmen, saying, "The water is ours." And he called the name of the well Esek [quarrel]; because they contended with him. And they digged another well, and they strove for that also. And he called the name of it Sitnah [hostility]. And he removed from thence, and digged another well; and for that they strove not. And he called the name of it Rehoboth; and he said: "For now the Lord hath made room for us, and we shall be fruitful in the land." And he went up from thence to Beer-sheba (Genesis 26:19-23)

Again Isaac continued in this place the Hebrew tradition of his father: "And he builded an altar there, and called upon the name of the Lord, and pitched his tent there; and there Isaac's servants digged a well" (Genesis 26: 25).

Pitching a tent, digging a well, and calling upon the name of the Most High God—all in one breath.

It is obvious why the forefathers of our people went to the Negev: this was the most sparsely settled and populated part of the country, as it is in our own days. The first immigrant from the country now called Iraq, which then went under the name of Haran, found in the Negev a free and empty expanse, such as he could not find in any part of the Promised Land. In his new home he had to engage in constructive work: the search for water and the planting of trees, and in that desolate expanse he comprehended the supreme unity of existence.

The spies whom Moses sent to examine the country also went up first to the Negev, and from there to Hebron. The first Canaanite ruler the Children of Israel met in their journey north was the King of Arad, who dwelt in the Negev.

Since the feet of the Patriarchs trod the soil of the Negev, many changes and transformations have passed over it. Its ruined cities are evidence of the efforts of generations, from the days of Abraham to the end of the Byzantine era in the seventh century, to settle this desert and make it flourish; in recent years, archeological surveys have revealed ancient settlements all over the area. The Arab conquest in the seventh century nullified the work of the Jewish and Nabatean settlers, however, and today there remains hardly a trace of the cities of the tribes of Judah and Simeon in the south and the Negev.

The Book of Joshua (15:21-32) lists the cities which fell to the lot of the tribe of Judah, toward the border of Edom southwards: Kabzeel, Eder, Jagur, Kinah, Dimonah, Adadah, Kedesh, Hazor, Ithnan, Ziph, Telem, Bealoth, Hazor, Hadattah, Kerioth, Hezron (which is Hazor), Amam, Shema, Moladah, Hazar-gaddah, Heshmon, Beth-pelet, Hazar-shual, Beer-sheba, Bisiothiah, Baalah, Iim, Ezem, Eltolad, Chesil, Hormah, Ziklag, Madmannah, Sansannah, Lebaoth, Shilhim, Ain, Rimmon.

The tribe of Simeon, which later occupied part of the territory of Judah, also inhabited some of these towns (Beer-sheba, Eltolad, Moladah, Hazar-shual, Ezem, Ziklag, Ain and Rimmon), but also had towns in the Negev where the men of Judah did not live: Bethul, Balah, Sheba, Beth-hamercaboth, Hazor-susah, Ether, Ashan (the two latter towns are also mentioned among the towns of Judah in the Shefelah—Joshua 15:42).

The Bible distinguishes six areas in the Negev: Negev-Arad—the Judean Desert from east of Beer-sheba to the Dead Sea; Negev Judah—the central Negev; Negev Ha-yerahmieli and Negev Hakeni—both apparently in the southern Negev; Negev Hakerethi—apparently the western Negev on the side of Philistia; Negev Kaleb—possibly a part of Negev Judah.

The prophets never reconciled themselves to the desolation of the Negev. Isaiah, the son of Amoz, prophesied:

The wilderness and the parched land shall be glad;
And the desert shall rejoice, and blossom as the
    rose. . . .
Then shall the lame man leap as a hart,
And the tongue of the dumb shall sing;
For in the wilderness shall waters break out,
And streams in the desert.
And the parched land shall become a pool,
And the thirsty ground springs of water. . . .
And a highway shall be there, and a way,
And it shall be called the way of holiness. . . .
But the redeemed shall walk there. (Isaiah 35:1-9)

Here the prophet outlined all the principal activities required for the development of the Negev, activities that are not yet out of date.

And the prophet Jeremiah said:

For thus saith the Lord: like as I have brought all this great evil upon this people, so will I bring upon them all the good that I have promised them. And fields shall be bought in this land, whereof ye say: It is deso-

193

late without man or beast; . . . Men shall buy fields for money, and subscribe the deeds, and seal them, and call witnesses, in the land of Benjamin, and in the places about Jerusalem, and in the cities of Judah, and in the cities of the hill-country, and in the cities of the Lowland, and in the cities of the South; for I will cause their captivity to return, saith the Lord. (Jeremiah 32:42-44)

In the Negev there were in ancient days the first mines, which increased the country's trade during the period of the early kings of Judah. Even the Pentateuch praised the "land whose stones are iron, and out of whose hills thou mayest dig brass" (Deuteronomy 8:9), and one of the latest of the prophets speaks of "mountains of brass" (Zechariah 6:1). In the mountains of Timna in the southern Negev King Solomon mined copper, which was smelted in the furnace he built in Ezion-Geber, as has been proved in our own day in the course of the excavations of Professor Nelson Glueck, the American Jewish archeologist. So plentiful was copper in Solomon's day that it is written of him: "And Solomon left all the vessels unweighed, because they were exceeding many; the weight of the brass could not be found out" (I Kings, 7:47), and the story of David mentions "brass and iron without weight . . . in abundance" (I Chronicles, 22:14). And indeed iron and copper deposits have been found in our own day in the Negev, although some of them were undoubtedly depleted in ancient times.

The ancients were also aware of the plentiful deposits of *hemar* (asphalt) to be found in the neighborhood of the Dead Sea ("now the vale of Sidim was full of pits of *hemar*"—Genesis 14:10) and knew how to make use of it.

The Negev was of particular importance even in ancient times because of the Red Sea Gulf at its southern end. This was the first outlet of the Jewish people to the sea. Three kings of the House of David attempted to reach the southern tip of the Negev and make Eilat the first Jewish port on the Red Sea: Solomon, Jehoshaphat, and Uzziah.

The road to Eilat on the Red Sea coast—the Arava—and the town itself first belonged to Edom, as the Pentateuch relates; "So we passed by from our brethren the children of Esau, that dwell in Seir, from the way of the Arabah, from Elath and from Ezion-Geber" (Deuteronomy 2:8). In David's time Edom was conquered: "And all the Edomites became servants to David" (II Samuel 8:14). David's heir King Solomon directed all his energies to increasing his country's wealth by peaceful means and hence appreciated the economic importance of Eilat: "And King Solomon made a navy of ships in Ezion-Geber, which is beside Eloth, on the shore of the Red Sea, in the land of Edom" (I Kings 9:26).

The division of the kingdom in the days of Rehoboam resulted in the loss of Eilat. But the fourth king after Rehoboam, Jehoshaphat the son of Asa, succeeded in making an alliance with Ahab, King of Israel, and was able in consequence to recapture Eilat and make another attempt to develop Jewish shipping after the manner of King Solomon.

After the death of Ahab, one of the greatest of the kings of Israel, the relations between Jehoshaphat, King of Judah, and Ahaziah, Ahab's son, deteriorated. Ahaziah too wished to have a share in the Red Sea shipping, but Jehoshaphat rejected this proffered partnership ("Then said Ahaziah the son of Ahab unto Jehoshaphat: 'Let my servants go with thy servants in the ships.' But Jehoshaphat would not" (I Kings 22:50). Judah was weakened by this quarrel, and Eilat again slipped out of Jewish hands. Four more generations passed before Amaziah, son of Joash, King of Judah, defeated Edom in the Valley of Salt and took Selah (capital of Edom). His son Uzziah (Azariah) rebuilt Eilat and restored it to Judah (II Kings 14:22). Uzziah, one of the greatest statesmen in Judah's history, maintained a friendly alliance with Jeroboam II, King of Israel and one of her greatest rulers, and both expanded the borders of their countries: Uzziah in the south and Jeroboam in the north.

King Uzziah was a great commander, successful in conquest and in settling the desert and making it flourish. In his days the Jewish army increased in strength; settlement and irrigation were fostered; a port was built at Eilat; and simultaneously with political and economic progress there was a remarkable development in spiritual and moral culture. In the days of Uzziah there arose the first great literary prophets: Amos, Hosea, and Isaiah, who bequeathed to the Jewish people and the whole of humanity teachings of righteousness, mercy, universal peace, brotherhood, and equality, and the vision of Jewish and human redemption in the latter days. It was not for nothing that Uzziah, unlike any other king of Judah or Israel, was privileged to have the story of his life and deeds written by the great prophet, Isaiah the son of Amoz.

Thanks to Uzziah's conquests and development works in the south and the Negev, Eilat remained in Jewish hands for three generations—during the days of Uzziah, Jotham, and Ahaz, kings of Judah.

Jotham, Uzziah's son, continued his father's development work and expanded the boundaries of his southern territories in the east: "Moreover he built cities in the

196

hill-country of Judah, and in the forests he built castles and towers. He fought also with the King of the children of Ammon, and prevailed against them" (II Chronicles, 27:4-5).

When the Kingdom of Israel was destroyed in the days of Hosea the son of Elah, the Kingdom of Judah was also weakened, and Rezin, King of Aram, restored Eilat to Edom, "and drove the Jews from Elath; and the Edomites came to Elath, and dwelt there, unto this day" (II Kings, 16:6).

In our own time, in March, 1949, the Israel Defense Forces entered Eilat and restored it to Israel. In place of the traditional boundaries from Dan to Beersheba, Israel's borders were extended about 250 kilometers south of Beersheba, and for the first time in our history the Jewish State borders on two seas: the Red Sea in the south and the Mediterranean in the west. From the standpoint of world transport, the Negev resembles the Suez Canal; it serves as a bridge between the world's two shipping regions: the Mediterranean route to the Atlantic Ocean, and the Red Sea route to the Indian and Pacific oceans.

The Negev has one other sea, of no great importance for transport, for it is a closed inland lake: the Dead Sea. However, it is unique, for it lies in the deepest cleft on the surface of the globe—about four hundred meters below sea level—and it is richer in salts and minerals than any other area in the world. It contains about two billion tons of potash, over twenty billion tons of magnesium chloride, over ten billion tons of sodium chloride, about six billion tons of calcium chloride, almost a billion tons of magnesium bromide, and other minerals. It is also rich in medicinal springs, which have not yet been properly explored but are undoubtedly of great potential benefit to health.

Since the expanses of the Negev were redeemed by the Israel Defense Forces, the Negev has been explored and investigated anew, although the researches have not yet gone far enough, and latent resources still outweigh those that have been revealed. It has turned out that copper and iron are not the only minerals to be found there. Numerous phosphate deposits, some of which are being exploited, have been discovered, from which uranium, the precious element required for atomic research, can be extracted. We have discovered gypsum, marble, and granite, deposits of first-quality glass sand, bituminous stone, kaolin, natural gas, and so forth. It cannot yet be said, however, that we have laid bare all the treasures hidden in the depths of the soil of this great desert. Detailed investigation is still required of the flora and fauna of the Negev, its climate and dew deposits, the quality of the soil and its geological structure.

The remarkable progress of the natural sciences during the last three hundred years has so far been concentrated mainly in the northern countries, i.e., in Europe and America, where there is no shortage of water and power resources: coal, oil, gas, waterfalls. Rain is plentiful in these countries almost all the year round, and their extensive deposits of coal and iron were the foundation for the great industrial revolution that took place in the nineteenth century.

As one of the few civilized peoples that have returned to their ancient Homeland in a subtropical and mainly arid country, we must concentrate on research projects that are not of vital importance for the northern peoples. Hence Israel's capacity for science and research will be tested in the Negev. Research alone, however, is not enough.

The triangle of the Negev is situated between two hos-

198

tile countries: Egypt and Jordan. Across its southwestern border stretches the Sinai Desert, and the Arabian Desert is on its eastern border. The Arabs have transformed more than one flourishing and populous country into a desert: the wasteland in the Arab states is no obstacle to their survival and independence. The small State of Israel, however, cannot long tolerate within its bounds a desert that takes up over half its territory. If the State does not put an end to the desert, the desert is likely to put an end to the State. The narrow strip between Jaffa and Haifa, fifteen to twenty-five kilometers wide, which contains the bulk of Israel's population, cannot survive for long without a large and firmly based population in the expanses of the south and the Negev.

By daring, creative initiative and physical labor, the pioneers among the Jewish people during the last three generations transformed the face of the land while it was yet under foreign rule, and paved the way for the establishment of the State of Israel. They brought fertility to the sands and the stony places, drained swamps, dug wells, planted vineyards and orchards, covered the hills with forests, built villages and cities, and developed industry and handicrafts. But their labors were limited to the northern half of western Palestine, and even within these limits they concentrated mainly on the coastal plain and the Jezreel and Jordan valleys, where the soil is generally fertile and adequate rain is more or less available. The southern half of the country remained desolate, as it had been for centuries, ever since the Arab conquest. Neither the Turks nor the British attempted to make this desert flourish, for they had no need to do so, and the Negev continued to lie under the curse of the prophet Jeremiah: "The cities of the South are shut up, and there is none to open them" (Jeremiah 13:19). After the issue of the Chamberlain Government's White Paper in 1939, the Jews were forbidden to obtain a foothold in the Negev and the greater part of the south.

Foreign rule and non-Jewish ownership of the land limited the areas in which we could settle. Among those who did much for settlement and the redemption of the soil before the rise of the State there were a number of farsighted personalities, who showed great skill in their efforts to acquire land under the difficult conditions of Ottoman rule and the Mandatory regime. Outstanding among them was Baron Edmond de Rothschild, that extraordinary man who emerged from assimilated French Jewry to devote all his life and a large part of his enormous wealth, in his profound love for the soil of the Homeland, to agricultural settlement. But the foreign, generally hostile regime and the obstructive laws were an obstacle to any attempt to plan for the country as a whole, and the dream of settlement in Trans-Jordan, for which Rothschild worked hard, evaporated under the pressure of political conditions. As for the south, all of it was in practice out of bounds for modern Jewish settlement. Thus the whole of the Jewish population was crowded together in the narrow strip between Jaffa and Haifa, with a few outlying districts stretching northward and southward.

The War of Independence placed at our disposal the whole soil of the State, from Metulla in the north to Eilat in the south. All of the lands of the south, to the west of the Armistice lines in the Hebron sector, and the whole of the Negev, from Beersheba to Eilat, have been restored to the young State. All legal and political hindrances to the settlement of the bulk of the country's lands have been removed—and the greater part of the soil of the new Israel is in the south and the Negev. The only remaining obstacle in the way of our expansion and settlement in the south derives from the hostility of nature: namely, the wasteland and the shortage of rain.

The great energy, the courage, and the constructive initiative of Jewish youth, and the scientific and technological capacity of Israel's scientists and research workers, will have to overcome these natural difficulties and develop the south and the Negev for large-scale settlement based on pasture, agriculture, handicrafts, mining and industry, fishing and shipping—exploiting all the resources of the scientific discoveries and technological progress of our day.

It is absolutely vital for the State of Israel, for both economic and security reasons, to move southward: to direct the country's water and rain, the young pioneers and the new immigrants, and most of the resources of the development budget, to the south; to uproot a considerable proportion of our workshops and factories and transfer them to the south; to move a number of our scientific and research institutions, dealing with the country's geography, soil structure, vegetation, climate, and natural resources, to the south. We must concentrate the attention of Israel's scientists and research workers on the investigation of the forces, known or latent, with whose aid we shall be able to make the lands of the south and the Negev thrive.

Without the settlement of the south and the Negev this country cannot be secure, and we shall not succeed in attaining economic independence. But these areas cannot be settled without the transformation of the facts of Nature, an accomplishment not beyond the capacity of science in our day or the pioneering energy of our youth. Science and pioneering will enable us to perform this miracle.

In fact, the whole of our achievement in this country is one of the wonders of history. There is nothing supernatural about it; miracles of the supernatural type are not wonderful at all—for if it is possible to create the globe and set it in endless motion around the sun, it is also possible to command the earth or the sun to stand still. Human reason has not yet succeeded—and it is doubtful whether it ever will succeed—in understanding the secret of creation and solving the riddle of existence and eternal renewal. The more human experience and reason learn of the world around us and within us, the more profound grows the riddle, and the farther we are from understanding the eternal secret. But man's experience grows constantly richer; his mastery of his environment and of himself continually increases; the instruments which he creates to increase his capacity to examine and understand nature, and in part to gain domination over it, grow more perfect; and the human horizon incessantly expands.

Surely the most wonderful and most powerful instrument through which man gains the mastery over nature is man himself. The potentialities latent in this wonderful being have no parallel among all the complex and marvelous instruments and machines that man has created. Only through an intuitive understanding of man's potentialities—which we call *halutziut* or pioneering—have we succeeded in our enterprise in this country, which seemed to be completely incompatible with all accepted laws and conventional concepts.

Who believed decades ago that Jews who for centuries had lived in towns, and for generations had been stran-

gers to labor and the soil, would become the builders of
a country? Who imagined that a people that had been
scattered and dispersed for over two thousand years
would reassemble in its ancient Homeland under foreign
occupation and in it renew its sovereign independence?
Who believed that a dead language, embalmed in hymns
and books of prayer, would once again become the living speech of a people which spoke a Babel of tongues?
Who dreamt that a people oppressed, degraded, and
helpless for generations would suddenly reveal a heroic
spirit and crush a hostile invader forty times its size?

The faith, bold and naïve at the same time, that the
early pioneers displayed eighty years ago, and the force
of the creative initiative they showed in establishing new
Jewish villages in the ancient, captive Homeland; the
pioneering impetus that grew steadily stronger in the
course of the last three generations until it achieved the
revival of the Jewish State and the brilliant victories of
the War of Independence; the daring involved in settling
tens of thousands of immigrants from backward countries, who for thousands of years had been foreign to the
fragrance of the fields, in the desolate wastes of the south;
the cultural, social, and economic transformations that
took place in the lives of hundreds of thousands of immigrants in two or three generations, transformations
unparalleled either in the life of our own people since its
beginnings or in that of any other people in our own day
—all these are the fruit of the great human miracle of our
modern history, which is nothing else but the profound
faith of man in his will power and capacity, and a burning
spiritual need to transform the natural order, as well as
the order of his own life, for the sake of the redeeming
vision.

By virtue of this miracle of *halutziut* our people resisted the habits acquired in the Diaspora and uprooted them, resisted political difficulties and overcame them, resisted the incitement and hostility of our neighbors and gained the victory, fought against the poverty and ruination of our country—and rebuilt its ruined places.

Now, in the very hour when we have gained free and sovereign control over all the lands and resources of the State, we have come face to face with the greatest difficulty: the curse of nature, the barrenness and desolation of the greater part of our soil.

The State, the nation, the youth, the men of science now confront the supreme test in the history of our progress toward independence and the renewal of our sovereignty. Only through a united effort by the State in planning and execution, by a people ready for a great voluntary effort, by a youth bold in spirit and inspired by a creative heroism, by scientists liberated from the bonds of conventional thought and capable of probing deep into the special problems of this country, shall we succeed in carrying out the great and momentous task of developing the south and the Negev.

It is only a conventional approach and conventional thought rooted in the past that have given the impression that the expanses of the Negev are condemned to remain desolate to all eternity. There are plentiful resources of water and power which we have not yet exploited, because we did not know the secret of their use. But it does not follow that what we did not know up to yesterday we shall not know tomorrow. The ground waters, springs, rivers, and brooks of our country are limited and scanty, nor have we as yet fully exploited even these. The Jordan waters flow down to the Dead Sea; a considerable proportion of the water of Lake Kinneret evaporates; and even the rains, plentiful in the north and scanty in the south, flow uselessly in large measure to the Mediterranean or the Dead Sea, without fully benefiting the thirsty soil. In addition, we waste a considerable part of the water at our disposal, especially in the northern part of the country, which has plentiful supplies. We have not yet succeeded in collecting all the rain water, so that it will not flow unused into the sea, or in making the most economical and efficient use possible of the water resources we possess.

But the great problem of supplying water to the expanses of the south and the Negev is that of extracting the salts from sea water. The great task that our science must achieve is the discovery of a cheap and practical method of desalting sea water, with which it will be possible to slake the thirst of the arid lands. In the United States of America, rich in mighty rivers and broad lakes, research and experiment have been conducted for years on the purification of sea water for the purpose of irrigating the deserts in the west. We are much more in need of this new and unlimited source of irrigation water than the United States, and it is not beyond the capacity of our scientists and technologists, if they devote their best efforts to research in this direction and receive all possible assistance from the State, to discover a cheap process for desalting sea water. The irrigation of the desert with purified sea water will appear a dream to many, but less than any country should Israel be afraid of "dreams" capable of transforming the natural order by the power of vision, science, and pioneering capacity; all that has been accomplished in this country is the result of such "dreams." And indeed considerable progress has been made.

The purification of sea water by a cheap process is not only a vital need for Israel; it is a necessity for the world. Hundreds of millions of the inhabitants of the great continent in which we live suffer from lack of food, but as yet only a small part of the earth's surface is tilled. In Asia and Africa, and in America too, there are enormous deserts which, with water for irrigation, could double and treble the world's harvests and supply food in plenty to tens of millions. If Israel succeeds in desalting the water of the sea, it will bring great benefits to the entire human race, and the task is not beyond the power of our scientists.

Science derives from two sources: the creative capacity of the human mind and the vital needs of society. The human mind does not deploy all its capacity except under the pressure of society's needs; without this pressure it invests its energy in other matters. These two factors are no less powerful in Israel than in any other country.

The problem of power is similarly important. Power is required for the utilization of water in all its forms, but not for that alone. The richer human culture becomes, and the more man's requirements multiply, the greater grows his need for power and energy. Primitive man used to consume up to 3,000 calories by eating food prepared for him by nature. After man learned to use fire and domesticate certain animals, he needed about 10,000 calories, in order to produce food for his livestock as well as for himself. Technical improvements and the manufacture of machines increased his daily consumption of energy. If we take into account machinery, aircraft, railways, lighting installations, and calculate the amount required per head, we shall find that in the United States man consumes an average of 160,000 calories of energy per day. If in Israel we wish to maintain a high level of culture—and we must aspire to secure a cultural level in our own country no lower than that of any other

—we must endeavor to create adequate sources of power to supply all the energy required by men, animals, and inanimate things; land, sea, and air transport, lighting and communications, machinery for all the branches of the economy and for all educational and cultural purposes.

Our scientists, therefore, must not only continue the studies and researches with which they were occupied abroad but devote themselves to those problems bearing on our country's natural resources and the things it must have to survive.

We are living on the eve of one of the greatest revolutions in the history of man and his mastery of nature: we stand face to face with the era of atomic energy. Although the principal sources of power in the most highly developed countries are coal, oil, and electricity, there is no doubt that in a few years man will harness the mighty and wonderful forces latent in the invisible atom for the purposes of industry, agriculture, and transport, as he has already utilized them for war. Although our country is in general poor in natural resources—and we are not yet fully aware of all that lies concealed in the depths of its soil—the utilization of atomic energy depends first on the capacity of the biological and psychological instrument known as the mind of man. And the instruments of this kind at our disposal are not inferior in quality and capacity to those at the disposal of the world's richest and most highly developed nations.

Shortly after the end of the War of Independence, a Scientific Council was set up in Israel, and an Atomic Energy Committee was established, which has devoted no little talent to this question and has had some measure of success. This Committee has reached agreement with the French and British Governments on the production of heavy water, one of the substances required for the de-

207

velopment of atomic energy. The principal producers of heavy water today are Norway and the United States, each possessing cheap electricity. Our young scientists have discovered by themselves how to make heavy water, although we are still far from producing it in considerable quantities.

The principal materials required for the production of atomic energy are uranium and thorium. Although, so far as we know, uranium does not exist in Israel in such large quantities as it does in the Congo and certain other countries, this precious element is not lacking in our country. Hence we are capable of building atomic reactors, since we possess the two principal requirements —uranium and heavy water—although we shall have to make considerable efforts in order to produce them, and it will take some time before we attain the goal. We must, however, mobilize the manpower required to educate enough physicists and technologists of high quality and to exploit the raw materials available, so that within the next ten years we may be able to produce atomic energy, which will open up new prospects for our economic development in general and the revival of the Negev in particular.

Albert Einstein's revolutionary discovery of the identity of matter and energy, and the research that laid bare the complex structure of the atom, have placed untold treasures of energy at the disposal of the human race. This wonderful achievement will not remain the heritage of the Great Powers alone, and the increased cooperation between scientists all over the world in atomic research is a good omen for our generation. It is not impossible for scientists in Israel to do for their own people what Einstein, Oppenheimer, and Teller—all three Jews —have done for the United States.

Atomic energy is not the only source of power that is destined to result in an inconceivable extension of the powers of man. The mightiest source of energy in our world, the source from which all animal and vegetable life is nourished, and only an infinitesimal part of which is as yet utilized by the human race, is the sun. Experts have calculated that the solar energy reaching the earth's surface in three days is equal to the quantity of energy that can be extracted by the consumption of all the deposits of coal, oil, natural gas, and peat on the face of the globe, as well as all the forests.

The Negev is most plentifully provided with this form of energy, for there are few cloudy or rainy days. So far no more than a drop out of this ocean of energy has been utilized by the plants we grow, whose secret is simply the absorption of solar energy by the process of photosynthesis. The Negev today derives less benefit than any other region from the absorption of the sun's rays by plants, but this energy can be transformed into an active, dynamic, and electrifying force. Even after all the uranium and thorium deposits disappear from the earth, solar energy will continue to reach us in almost unlimited quantities, and our scientists and technologists must discover the most effective means for putting even a very small part of this tremendous energy to work for the growing and manifold needs of our variegated economy. It is not impossible that we may be able to use solar energy to purify sea water for the purpose of irrigating the vast wastes of the south and the Negev.

The use of atomic power and solar energy, the production of electric power with the help of the winds and the waves, the exploitation of the plentiful natural resources of the Dead Sea, the damming of the floods that flow uselessly into the sea and the building of reservoirs to

209

collect the water for drinking, irrigation, and other development works, the discovery of metal mines, marble and granite, and the like—all these are the concern of physicists, geologists, chemists, and engineers. But the latent energy of nature, hidden in the womb of earth, in the waterfalls, the atom, and the sun, will not be sufficient unless we are able to utilize the most precious energy of all: the moral and spiritual energy latent in man, in the recesses of his divine, mysterious being, whose secret no one knows, but whose existence, force, activity, and influence every man can recognize. This wonderful energy has found expression among us, both in its moral and in its intellectual power, not less than in any other human society; it is only through this energy that the miracle of our survival in exile for two thousand years and the miracle of our revival in our own days have taken place; it is through it alone that our forefathers in days of old and our youth in our own generation have performed deeds in this little country that have no parallel in human history.

Not nature, which has remained unchanged for millions of years, but the ever-soaring spirit of man has transformed the face of the globe. By the power of his thought and the boldness of his spirit man extends his domination over nature, reveals its secrets, subordinates it to his material and spiritual needs. And in the whole of human history there is no more mighty expression of the power of the spirit to face difficulties, obstacles, tribulations, and dangers than that which has been revealed in the history of the Jewish people from its beginning in the days of the Patriarchs until this day.

Fifteen years ago a new chapter was opened in the history of this extraordinary people. The revival of Jewish sovereignty brought the Jewish people face to face with its destiny, without any intervening barrier. Immediately on the proclamation of its independence the young State had to face the attack of five of its neighbors—and gained the victory. Israel cannot survive without strength and power, so long as the human race is divided into warring blocs and nation lifts up sword against nation. But the profound truth of the supremacy of the spirit, the most incontrovertible proof of which is the long history and the manifold experiences of the Jewish people, remains unchallenged. It is on this truth that the faith of the Jewish people in its future is based. The supreme test of Israel in our generation lies, not in its struggle with hostile forces without, but in its success in gaining domination, through science and pioneering, over the wastelands of its country in the south and the Negev.

Chapter Thirteen
Towards a New World

Israel's future will be determined first of all by our success in developing our own resources, but we have never lost sight of the importance of maintaining and strengthening our position in the family of nations. The aims of our foreign policy are: the consolidation of our security; the ingathering of the exiles; the welfare of world Jewry and the liberty of all Jews to join us in the Homeland; cooperation with new nations as far as lies within our power; and support for world peace. Something more should be said of the last two points: Israel's contribution to the advancement of the nations and to the strengthening of peace and brotherhood among men.

We are on the threshold of a new and unprecedented era in the annals of mankind. Nations of every size, long under foreign rule, some with ancient cultures, others primitive for centuries, are casting off the yoke and grasping independence. The day cannot be far off when all peoples, no matter what their color, race, or culture, will

212

be members in the family of man, equal in rights, sovereign, and free.

Yet all nations, whatever their strength or stature, are growing more and more dependent upon each other. There is hardly a state, large, rich, and powerful though it be, that can do without the co-operation and support of others.

Differences between single states and blocs are still many and sharp. And the fear of war is with us yet, like none man has ever known. In recent years his genius has devised frightful weapons that could wipe out the whole, or the best part, of civilization. In spite of that—perhaps because of it—the consciousness grows of the imperious need to safeguard peace and human unity, and of the common destiny of all nations. Wittingly or unwittingly, man seeks political and cultural unity.

Poor and primitive peoples no longer wish to endure their wretched state. Rich and advanced peoples are beginning more and more to understand that the chasm that divides the sated from the starving, the rich in material and spiritual things from the recourseless and ignorant, must speedily be bridged.

In the last five hundred years, Europe extended its mastery over almost the whole earth—except for Japan, China, Persia, and Ethiopia (for America and Australia, the continents of the New World, were occupied and settled mainly by European immigrants). This was not done by military force alone; it was undoubtedly the consequence of the rising cultural and economic superiority of the European peoples, their vigor and initiative in discovering and colonizing new territory, the economic progress of the Industrial Revolution, the advance of pure and applied natural sciences, and better technology. These gave Europe, America, and Australia the modern leadership of mankind, and it will not be easy for the new states to equal these achievements.

This superiority does not stem from a monopoly of hereditary talent. The cultural and economic gap between Europe, America, and Australia and the peoples of Asia and Africa is not ordained by an immutable law of nature. In the last few generations we have seen the Japanese, divorced from Europe and America until the middle of the nineteenth century, as distant from the West's scientific and technological achievements as East is from West, absorb in a brief spell of years much of what European civilization had produced. Today the Japanese are the peers, in culture, scientific education, and technological capacity, of the most highly developed Westerners. A casual glance at history shows that the peoples of Europe were not always in the van of culture; thousands of years ago science and technology were cradled in Africa and Asia, which today, in their civilization, are inferior to the West. It has been rightly said that if a Martian had come to this earth anything from three thousand to five hundred years before the Common Era he would have averred that the peoples of the Middle East were the noblest of earthlings, and between fifteen and five centuries ago the Chinese and Indians would have been his choice.

Over five thousand years ago, in the northeast corner of Africa, in the Nile Valley, the spirit of man registered its first exploits in science and art, the understanding of nature and the control of the elements. Europe was still illiterate when a rich culture came into being in the Middle East and in China, and the wise men of Egypt and Babylon hit upon crucial truths of astronomy, medicine, and chemistry, geometry and planned agriculture. The religions that dwell in the hearts of hundreds of millions on earth originated in Asia: Judaism, Hinduism, Buddhism, Christianity, and Islam. Moses the Hebrew, Confucius and Lao-tzu of China, the Hindu Buddha, Iranian Zoroaster, Jesus of Nazareth, the Arab Mohammed are universally revered. Civilization still bears the impress of the legislators, prophets, sages, and philosophers of western and eastern Asia, of Israel, of China and India, of Persia and Arabia. The great thinkers of Greece, pre-eminent twenty-five centuries ago in scientific and philosophic thought, drew their doctrines from the Middle East and India. Until the mid-sixteenth century, India knew next to nothing of the European peoples and had nothing to learn from them; she herself was the cultural and educational focus of the Far Eastern nations: Japan, Korea and Siam, Tibet and Burma. The political, economic, and cultural greatness of Europe came only in the last four or five centuries, after Vasco da Gama sailed around the southernmost cape of Africa to reach India, and Columbus, setting out from Spain on a western voyage to the subcontinent, unwittingly discovered the New World on his way.

The Mediterranean basin was for long central in mankind's cultural and spiritual and economic progress, of which Israel, Greece, and Rome were in ancient days the threefold instrument. As European immigrants colonized America, the pendulum swung to the shores of the Atlantic, and there the power of arms, material wealth, and superiority in science and technology built a far-reaching ascendancy. Now two great powers bestride the globe and are wrestling for hegemony: the United States of America and the Russian empire, which Lenin, a tactical genius, called the Soviet Union.

The United States and the Soviet Union were allied in the Second World War, and with their combined forces crushed the Nazi tyrant; Britain, France, and other allies, including Jewish units from Palestine some 30,000 strong, were at their side. But victory was only too soon dogged by conflicts between the West and Russia, and in Poland, Rumania, Czechoslovakia, Bulgaria, Hungary, Albania, and East Germany the Communist party came to power. So were produced the Communist bloc and the free bloc of the West; friction grew; the Cold War had begun.

Leaders in the Cold War are two great powers—the United States, which believes in democratic liberty, and the Soviet Union, which maintains a Communist regime. Thus is apparently fulfilled the prophecy of that great political thinker Alexis de Tocqueville, who foretold this confrontation 125 years ago in his penetrating book on American democracy. In 1835 De Tocqueville wrote, after a stay in the United States:

There are, at the present time, two great nations in the world which seem to tend toward the same end, although they started from different points: I allude to the Russians and the Americans. Both of them have grown up unnoticed; and while the attention of mankind was directed elsewhere, they have suddenly assumed a most prominent place among the nations; and the world learned of their existence and their greatness at almost the same time.

All other nations seem to have nearly reached their natural limits, and only to be charged with the maintenance of their power; but these are still in the act of growth; all the others are stopped, or continue to advance with extreme difficulty; these are proceeding with ease and with celerity along a path to which the human eye can assign no term. The American struggles against the natural obstacles which oppose him; the adversaries of the Russian are men; the former combats the wilderness and savage life; the latter, civilization with all its weapons and its arts; the conquests of the one are therefore gained by the ploughshare; those of the other by the sword. The Anglo-American relies upon personal interest to accomplish his ends, and gives free scope to the unguided exertions and common sense of the citizens; the Russian centres all the authority of society in a single arm; the principal instrument of the former is freedom; of the latter servitude. Their starting-point is different, and their courses are not the same; yet each of them seems to be marked out by the will of Heaven to sway the destinies of half the globe.

When De Tocqueville wrote, America had a population of only 15 million; today she has more than 180 million. The population of the Soviet Union is over 218 million; the first census ever taken in Russia, in February, 1897, gave 129,800,000, including Finland; in 1723, under Peter the Great, the estimate was 14 million. The United States has an area of almost nine and a half million square kilometers, the Soviet Union 22.4 million, most of it annexed after De Tocqueville's book appeared.

His prescience was astonishing; nearly all he said has come true. Like most of his contemporaries, he ascribed no importance to Asia and Africa or their many peoples; for him they were not an independent factor, and indeed in his lifetime they hardly played an independent role in world affairs or affected the course of history. But today, and even more hereafter, those peoples are destined to exert a powerful influence not only in their own countries but on the future of humanity. De Tocqueville's analysis of the character and importance of the two great powers is, however, largely unimpeachable still, even if

217

America's conquests are no longer achieved by the plow, or Russia's by the sword.

In military strength the two are fairly level, and in technological capacity likewise, though the United States is wealthier and workers there enjoy a much higher standard of living than their Soviet counterparts. Both command a shattering weapon, first developed by the United States during the Second World War: the atom bomb, which since then has been "improved"; for both, and Britain too, now boast the hydrogen bomb, a thousand-fold more devastating. Is it any wonder that the world is haunted by the insistent dread of a frightful Third World War, fought with atomic armaments, likely to decimate mankind and blot out highly civilized and densely populous lands?

Although logically it is hardly conceivable that either of the "Cold Warriors" should start such horror, the anxiety cannot be allayed entirely. Each side knows the other can pulverize it; in a war between the two, victory is nearly impossible and mutual destruction certain. Each is capable of swiftly destroying its rival, and each, beyond the shadow of a doubt, is aware of it. A world war cannot, then, be thought likely, yet it is difficult to imagine that the Cold War will end, for it is a critical duel, with the souls of the peoples of Asia and Africa at stake, the souls of the greater part of humanity, and a part that takes on daily added status and meaning in international affairs.

De Tocqueville saw only two camps and, not without reason, personified them in America and Russia. Today, they are the peoples of western Europe and the United States on the one hand, and on the other the Communist bloc, led by Russia and comprising the peoples of eastern Europe. But a third camp, which did not visibly exist in his time, is swiftly growing. The peoples ruled by Europe for three centuries are now becoming free, and those that had ruled them, Britain and France especially, have given their consent; in Asia the process is almost consummated. Communist China, too, which in form belongs to the Communist bloc, tends to chart her course independently, and there is little doubt that her subordination to the Kremlin, if indeed it ever existed, will be constantly weakened and in course of time disappear entirely.

For thousands of years, the Chinese harbored a feeling of superiority over other peoples, undiminished by internecine strife or foreign invasion. This was inherited by Chinese Communism, which is striving, not without success, to attain modern standards of economic and cultural advancement. Diligent to a degree equal to any in the world, the Chinese are bound to realize that ambition, and soon. At the end of the last century, the Japanese succeeded in the effort and the Chinese are as persevering and as talented. The recent rate of natural increase (twenty-three per thousand) suggests that China will have a population of a billion in twenty years.

The country is a great riddle, which no outsider, probably not even any of its own leaders, can solve with certainty now. Two thousand years ago the Chinese knew nothing of the outside world; they regarded themselves as the whole of civilization. Nowadays, not even the largest and most populous of countries—and in population China comes first on earth—can ignore the rest, for there is a growing interdependence among the nations. China surely understands that she cannot do as she wishes. There are economic and cultural, political and military factors greater and stronger than herself. She too depends on them, as others depend on her, and, at least in public, she favors ties with the Soviet Union.

But there is no doubt that she alarms her neighbors in Asia, even India with a population of more than 440 million, and may provoke concern within the Soviet Union, for her population is multiplying fantastically, and great tracts of Russia, close to her borders, are almost empty. Patently, China will not join the democratic nations, but there is a strong likelihood that she will not follow in the Soviet footsteps. Without a doubt, she will try as energetically as the two Western blocs—for, to China, Russia is also of the West—to gain the adherence of the Asian and African peoples who are now or are soon to become independent, and in that regard she enjoys certain advantages over the Soviet Union.

Dividing the world into committed nations, in the Communist bloc on the one hand and in NATO on the other, and the uncommitted, we find this: The Warsaw Pact of the Soviet Union and its allies in Europe embraces 306,000,000 souls; add China and her Communist neighbors (700,000,000), and the figure comes to 1,006,000,000. NATO takes in populations of 191,830,000 in the United States and Canada, and 236,541,000 in western Europe, 428,371,000 in all. As for the uncommitted nations, there are: 65,258,000 in Europe, 198,170,000 in Latin America, 231,000,000 in Africa, 897,260,000 in Asia, and 15,800,000 in Oceania (Australia, New Zealand and other islands), 1,407,488,000 in all.

Of course, these figures by no means reflect precisely the number of Communists, true democrats, and neutrals. Within the NATO membership there are several millions with Communist sympathies. In the Communist bloc, outside the Soviet Union, the great majority are not Communists. And not all "neutrals" are really so: India, for instance, belongs to the British Commonwealth. In Egypt there is a dictatorial regime, anti-Communist at

220

home but supporting the Soviet Union faithfully in international issues. Guinea has a quasi-Communist regime; Pakistan, a member of CENTO closely linked with the United States, is under military rule. So to classify nations as committed, uncommitted, and "neutral" is no reflection of the opinions and outlooks of their peoples, but only of the attitudes of the rulers, a fact which accentuates the Cold War, that ideological, political, and propaganda struggle for the souls of nations.

The competition between the Communist bloc and the democratic West, and the independent international activity of China, undoubtedly disturb relations between states and heighten global tensions, even if we do not believe an atomic world war probable. They allow conscienceless dictators, without any political and social creed, to incite and subvert among their neighbors and extract from each side "aid and comfort" for their troublemaking. An outstanding example is Nasser, who persecutes Communists at home and accepts military and financial help from the Soviet Union, joins the "anti-imperialist" chorus of the Communist bloc, and simultaneously wheedles extensive financial assistance from the United States, in Kremlin jargon the "arch-imperialistic power." Nor for an instant does he slacken his scheming to dominate his neighbors by force, and to undermine independent Arab states in the Middle East and in North Africa.

It is not, however, inter-bloc rivalry in itself that is the central problem, but the state of things that gives it dangerous explosive force: the tremendous gap between the old world and new Asia and Africa. That is the crucial stumbling block. Nations are gaining freedom, but independence alone does not solve economic, social, and educational problems; on the contrary, it aggravates them, laying on the young states burdens they can hardly bear unaided, confronting them with urgent tasks they do not have the resources or the trained manpower to perform.

But we must distinguish between Asia and Africa. Most Asian nations have a long tradition of history and culture; in antiquity and in medieval times they excelled the Europeans—except for classical and Hellenistic Greece—in learning and culture, science and philosophy.

Japan is not behind Europe or the United States in know-how and technology, though her standard of living is lower.

China, not content with a distinguished past, is making a resolute effort to overtake the scientifically and technologically advanced Soviet Union. The speed of her development is much faster than Communist Russia's since 1917, and some authorities predict she will draw level in the next decade.

As far back as three millennia ago, India created a poetic, religious, and metaphysical literature—Vedas, Brahmanas and Upanishads—and a magnificent body of epic poetry. Her influence in the ancient world may be equated with that of Israel and Greece. She produced, as she still produces, illustrious personalities, original thinkers, and talented statesmen like King Asoka in the third century B.C.E. Of their number was one of the greatest men in history, Siddhartha Gautama, known as the Buddha, the enlightened or awakened one, who bequeathed to the peoples of eastern Asia an advanced and ethical theory of life, in no way dependent on "divine revelation" and the supernatural, but founded on human reason, a profound contemplation of the nature of

222

man and the universe, and aspiration to a life of purity, justice, mercy, and truth.

The pressing problems of India are illiteracy, disease, and mass poverty, especially in the villages, of which there are 560,000, containing over 80 per cent of the population. The average income per capita is seventy dollars a year. The average expectation of life is among the lowest in the world: thirty-two years for men and only thirty-one for women, although in almost all countries women are the longer-lived; infantile mortality, 185 per thousand, is the highest in the world. The Government, under Nehru, is making strenuous efforts to industrialize the country and to carry out five-year development plans, with the aid of the United States, West Germany, the Soviet Union, Britain, and France. Vinove Bhava, one of Gandhi's disciples, helped by Jayaprakash Narayan, a former leader of the Socialist party, started the Bhoodan movement, which seeks free gifts of land for landless villagers from owners of large estates. Nehru has proclaimed India's neutrality *vis-à-vis* the two world blocs, but this has not prevented grave conflicts with China; he claims that China has occupied large stretches of Indian territory along the common border, and the argument is still unsettled. His quarrel with Pakistan regarding the almost wholly Moslem Kashmir also persists.

Burma was for ages an independent kingdom, and the teachings of the Buddha reached it in the ninth century. Unlike India, Pakistan, and Ceylon, which joined the British Commonwealth after independence, Burma stands alone.

Persia, which in race and language is akin to Aryan India, is also a country of immemorial civilization, which has produced conquerors and kings distinguished not

223

only for valor and statesmanship but for nobility of character. Such was Cyrus the Great, founder of the great Persian Empire in the mid-sixth century B.C.E., magnanimous and friendly to the conquered, the model of Alexander the Great. Cyrus won the respect and affection of all peoples subject to his rule. The Persians called him "Father," the Greeks in his dominions regarded him as a great ruler and legislator, and the Jews described him as a Messiah of the Lord. For Cyrus vouchsafed the first Return to Zion:

Now in the first year of Cyrus king of Persia . . . he made a proclamation throughout all his kingdom, and put it also in writing, saying: "Thus saith Cyrus king of Persia: All the kingdoms of the earth hath the Lord, the God of heaven, given me; and He hath charged me to build Him a house in Jerusalem, which is in Judah. Whosoever there is among you of all His people—the Lord his God be with him—let him go up." (II Chronicles 36:22-23 and Ezra 1:1-3)

Persia's nearness to powerful Russia again and again jeopardized her independence, but it did not undo it, and she is celebrating in sovereignty the 2,500th anniversary of the accession of Cyrus. In a way, echoing Isaiah, it is a Jewish occasion:

Thus saith the Lord to His anointed,
To Cyrus, whose right hand I have holden,
To subdue nations before him,
And to loose the loins of kings;
To open the doors before him,
And that the gates may not be shut:

I will go before thee,
And make the crooked places straight. (Isaiah 45:1-2)

Judged by how they shaped the history of the old world, the other lands of Asia yield pride of place to a vast wilderness at the southwestern extremity of the continent; its inhabitants were practically unknown until the coming of Mohammed, Prophet of Islam, in the seventh century. The Arab tribes worshiped idols, but there were many Jewish tribes and Christians in Arabia; in his travels between Mecca and Damascus, Mohammed would converse with men of both faiths, and so there came to him the idea of the One and Only God. In his fortieth year—he was born in Mecca about 580 A.D.— he became convinced that it was his mission to bring the tidings of the One God to his people and to the whole world. At first he preached to his wife and kinsfolk, but the townsmen mocked at him and his doctrines, and in 622 he fled to Yatrib, later known as Medina; Moslem chronology begins then, being based on the Hejira— Mohammed's flight.

Here, openly and boldly, he proselytized, and within the eleven remaining years of his life the entire Arabian Peninsula adopted his religion. Unlike Christianity, Islam did not distinguish between God and Caesar; from the very start it was both religion and state: faith in the One God and the state of God's messenger. It united the Arab tribes by persuasion and by the sword. Of the three Jewish tribes that would not conform, two had to flee Arabia and the third was butchered. The Prophet's death did not lessen the victorious thrust of the new faith. No other gospel ever spread so swiftly and penetrated so deep. First Palestine and Syria were overrun; Iraq and

225

Persia were taken and their peoples converted by force, though Persia at least kept her native tongue. By the beginning of the eighth century, North Africa as far as the Atlantic Ocean was in Arab hands; the conquered peoples were obliged to accept Islam, and, extraordinarily, they accepted Arabic with it and forgot their own speech.

In Asia, the conquests and conversions went beyond Persia as far as Afghanistan and India. From India, in the sixteenth century, Islam filtered into Indonesia, now the most populous Moslem country in the world.

From North Africa again, Islam moved south to British and French Sudan, Mauretania, Senegal, Chad, Guinea, Northern Nigeria, the Somalilands, Eritrea, and the farthest points of East Africa,

In western Europe Christianity prevailed, and the Moslems were expelled from Spain; but the Moslem Turks entrenched themselves firmly at the southeastern limit of Europe in the mid-fourteenth century, and in 1453 they took Constantinople from the Byzantines, and they hold it still.

As Africa gains freedom, the number of Moslem states will grow, and, taking into account North Africa, where Islam and Arabic have mastery, the world power of Mohammed's creed must rise. Omitting the Moslem territories in central Asia, which are part of the Soviet Union, there are now 29 independent Moslem states, with a total of some 336 million souls, 74 million in Africa and 262 million in Asia. Although in some, such as Turkey, Iran, and most of the former French colonies in Africa, religion is not the decisive factor in the policy of governments, the bonds that hold the Moslem lands together are much stronger than the ties between the Christian or even the Catholic lands.

Few peoples in Africa, on the other hand, have a continuous history and a long tradition. North Africa was utterly severed from its past by the Moslem conquest. Colonists from Holland, who settled in South Africa, were in two hundred years seemingly transformed into a new nation, all spiritual ties with the mother country broken, and they possess today an area of 1,223,400 square kilometers, with a density of only twelve to the square kilometer. Some 14 per cent of the population are white, and alone enjoy civil rights; some twelve million Bantus enjoy none, but do most of the work, so that the white economy depends entirely on an underprivileged majority.

The Black African countries are more in the nature of geographical concepts, their frontiers determined by European conquerors, than territories with common national and linguistic characteristics, a common political history, and a cultural tradition. There are in them many Indians and a considerable number of Syrians and Lebanese, who handle almost all the trade.

As we have seen, there was only one area in Africa—the Nile Valley, in the north—that played a cultural role of the first importance for thousands of years. For over 2,500 years, however, Egypt suffered foreign conquest—Persian, Greek, and Roman. In the seventh century the Arabs wiped out her past and language, and her own culture ended. Carthage, also important in North Africa, was built, where Tunis stands today, in 850 B.C.E. by men from Tyre and Sidon, who spoke an Hebraic dialect.

Moses is the only great personality of African birth with enduring influence in cultural history and spiritual development, and even he was only a third-generation African, of a family that had gone down to Egypt from the country of the Hebrews, the Land of Israel, in the days of Joseph, thirty-three centuries ago.

Judaism, first of all great faiths and heritage of Jewry alone, appeared in Europe, Africa, America, and Australia only after the Dispersion. Christianity, also born in the Land of Israel, advanced primarily among the peoples of Europe and their offspring in America and Australia. Except for the Philippines, there is not a single independent Christian country in Asia, and until Dutch settlement in South Africa, Ethiopia was the only one in the Black Continent. By tradition, Ethiopia's kings are scions of King Solomon and the Queen of Sheba, but the nation was conquered for Christianity in the fourth century C.E., and in the sixth century (539 C.E.) Ethiopia overthrew the Jewish kingdom of Yosef Du-Navos in Yemen.

Only with European penetration in the second half of the nineteenth century did Christianity find its way into Black Africa.

Judaism gave birth to Christianity and afterwards to Islam, and the three covered the globe, but if we exclude the Soviet Union, which is atheist—for all its many Christian, Moslem, and Jewish believers—we find only one Jewish State in the world, in Asia, with a population of two millions; 21 Moslem states, in Asia and Africa, with a total of 370 million; and 62 Christian states, with a total of 923,765,000. But in Asia alone, apart from Asiatic Russia, there are 13 countries neither Christian nor Moslem, with a total of 1,294,600,000, more than all the Christian, Moslem, and Jewish states put together, not counting parts of Asia and Africa not yet independent and predominantly Christian and Moslem in faith. In every Christian, Moslem, or Jewish country there are of course many followers of the other faiths, but the number of Jews, Christians, and Moslems in other Asian countries is small by comparison. This means that Judaism,

228

both in its original and in its Christian and Moslem forms, failed to touch nearly half the human race, as concentrated in Asia, from India to Japan.

To traverse Africa in the ninth century beyond the southern limit of the Sahara Desert required fortitude only a few outstanding men possessed. Now anyone can fly to any corner of Africa in a few hours. Anywhere in Europe, America, or Australia you can tune in your radio and hear what Asia and Africa are saying and doing. Modern means of transportation and communication have cut down distances, brought people closer together, and turned the earth, once an uncemented mosaic of different and divided countries, into a single integrated and interdependent world. They have encouraged backward and seemingly helpless peoples to revolt against foreign rule and gain independence by force or negotiation. That is the secret of the tremendous political revolution in human history through which we are living. But independence, which will certainly come to all peoples, does not remove or reduce the vast differences in wealth, culture, health, and life expectancy between the ancient continents of Asia and Africa, and Europe, America, and Australia. Those who have now won, or are soon to win, freedom are aware of this gulf; they can understand that independence by itself does not solve their problems, but is only a key to the urgent and onerous task of lifting themselves out of the depths of ignorance, poverty, and disease. The common destiny of the human race, ever more evident with the shortening of space, has made the bridging of the gulf a universal problem. It is the duty of rich, developed, and progressive nations to do their utmost to succor the poor and backward. And this very duty has become a source of rivalry between the blocs of East and West, between democracy and Socialism on the one hand and totalitarian Communism on the other.

The peoples of Africa, Latin America, and Australia, most of Asia, and some of Europe—half mankind—belong to neither bloc. Of the other half, more than two-thirds live under Communist and less than a third under democratic rule, a few under Socialist but most under non-Socialist governments. The peoples of Europe, Australia, and most of Latin America—almost 300,000,000 souls outside any bloc—are by nature lovers of human freedom and most of them enjoy more or less progressive and democratic regimes. In certain European countries, Scandinavia, Austria, Iceland, and Switzerland, the Socialists rule alone or in coalition; in other countries they are close to power. There are Socialist movements in several Asian countries, but only in Nepal has there been a temporary Socialist government. The army rules in Pakistan, Iraq, Egypt, Sudan, and Indonesia. Democracy in India depends largely on the authority of one great man, Nehru. So we can understand the struggle for the souls of the Asian and African peoples, who, for lack of democratic traditions, sometimes any significant tradition of government, vacillate between the two extremes. Few non-committed nations tend positively toward Communism, but all are interested in material and cultural aid, and its source can be decisive. There are also rulers with dreams of dominating their neighbors. They are thus clients of the Communist bloc, which—for its own ends of hegemony—is ready to help dictators gain power over free peoples; a notable example is Egypt, where the military junta, which persecutes Egyptian Communists, is a devoted, or subservient, ally of the Soviet Union.

Most of the emergent states of Asia and Africa still lack the basic things: sanitation, elementary education, crop expansion to avert starvation, clean drinking water and irrigation, a modicum of industrial development, the casting out of rampant corruption, and upright and competent administration. For all this, they need external aid. Only small groups have a specific social or political outlook, and personal rivalry is likely to upset any orderly regime, as it did in the Congo and Laos. Independence can be got or given overnight, but it may take the labor of generations to found a tranquil national life and supply the people's wants. The events in the Congo, demonstrating international interdependence, are a grave warning to the free nations. Why should anyone in Europe, America, Asia, or Australia have cared who ran this new state? But it is fatally wrong to imagine that this was only a clash between two aspirants to power; the real, though covert, struggle is between the United Nations, enjoined to preserve world peace and the law of nations, and dictatorial violence that sought to impose its will by force on the people of the Congo and their neighbors.

There are Congo tribes which only fifty years ago were cannibals, and the world neither knew nor heeded. Today the world has been shaken by a conflict over power in that same country. For in these fifty years a world formerly fragmented by distances has become one—though not yet united—and whatever happens in one country now affects all the others.

And we Jews in our Homeland must ask ourselves: Can Israel assist in the progress and development of Asia and Africa? For Israel it is both a moral and a political issue, and from both aspects there is no doubt that Israel must look upon such aid as a historical mission, as necessary for Israel as it is beneficial to those we help.

From the start of our State, before the tide of independence swept over Africa, our Government deemed it a principal aim of foreign policy to form links with the peoples of Asia and help their development forward as far as it could, within the limits of our modest economic and technical resources. Now that most of Black Africa is self-governing, it needs and seeks that co-operation, ancient Ethiopia no less than infant states, and in some of them, relatively speaking, Israel has done a fair amount.

The growing number of the new countries and the massive assets and trained manpower they demand raise some doubt whether it is within Israel's reach to render a sizable measure of help. She is still, and for years will be, herself in need of aid from world Jewry and support from her friends abroad. No other country has such menacing problems of security. The Jewish people in Israel is still more potentially than actually a nation. Post-state immigrants have not yet merged wholly into the new nationhood, its economy, its Hebrew culture. Our scant resources are not enough for existence and urgent development in Galilee, the south, and the Negev, for the consolidation of new settlements; and swifter strides toward economic independence are our immediate need. What, then, can Israel contribute to the new countries in Asia and Africa and how?

The simple and truthful answer is: By what she does for herself in her own country.

Israel stands at the crossroads of Asia, Africa, and Europe. She emerged in western Asia four thousand years ago, when the the Middle East was the cradle and center of civilization; in antiquity she endowed mankind with an immortal faith and literature, and thereafter has rubbed shoulders with many peoples in all continents. In the Middle Ages the Jews were concentrated in Asia Minor and North Africa; in the thirteenth century Jewry in Europe began to expand, by 1880 over 88 per cent of it lived there, and by the outbreak of the Second World War it had laid foundations for the Jewish State.

More than a million immigrants have settled in new Israel, rather less than half from Europe and America, more than half from Asia and Africa. They spoke a medley of tongues; their cultural standards, their original customs, differed vastly. Of that portion of the Land of Israel which is within the borders of the Jewish State, the greater part is desolate wilderness, partly because of man's misdeeds in foreign, and mainly Arab, conquests, and partly through nature's doing.

In Israel the problems of the modern world—the closing of the economic and cultural gap between the rich and politically conscious and the poor and undeveloped —are being solved on a small scale. Barren soil is being fertilized and output increased, to provide a growing population with comfort. Communities far apart in language and history, in culture and economy, are being made into one uniform nation, enjoying the cultural standard and the way of living of enlightened and advanced countries. Israel is sowing the desert, rooting out diseases endemic among immigrants from backward lands, so that in average life expectancy she is now in the front rank.

She is creating new social patterns, founded on mutual assistance and co-operation, without deprivation or discrimination. She is training an army dedicated not only to protecting her frontiers but to integrating newcomers and conquering the desert. She maintains a stable democratic regime, guaranteeing the maximum degree of civic freedom, providing progressively improving public health and educational services. She fosters the ideal of labor, making the workingman a productive and progressive force in society. She brings up her youth to play everywhere a pioneering role. She applies her energies to science and research, for their own sake and so that their discoveries may benefit health, economic development, security, and reclamation. In all this, her paramount aim is the advancement of man.

All are essential tasks, vital to Israel's future, security, and progress, but by discharging them for her own advantage Israel by indirection helps the new states to the best effect and widest extent: *by being a model and example.* Only during the past few years has Israel attracted the finest of the young leaders of Asia and Africa, from the Philippines and Japan, Cambodia and Burma, Nepal and India, Nigeria and Ghana, Liberia and Ethiopia, Tanganyika and Kenya, Congo and Chad, Guinea and the Ivory Coast, and many more, to study cooperation and agricultural settlement, military organization, development areas, the labor movement, scientific institutions. They have not come because Israel is powerful and rich, but because the new states regard her as a suitable and instructive specimen of a country that is trying, with no little success, to solve problems that concern old and new in Asia and Africa and also in Latin America. The changes we have produced in the economic, social, and cultural structure of our ingathered people and the landscape and economy of the land are those that most Asian and African nations want. From us, more perhaps than from many others, they can learn how feasible and profitable such changes are, and how to bring them about at home.

The history of our people, our ancient past, our dispersion among the nations, our participation in the progress of recent centuries (as well as our not inconsiderable contribution to that progress), our settlement in the ancient and impoverished Homeland, the inexorable imperative and blessing of destiny—these have compelled us to undertake the arduous and revolutionary tasks of the last three generations. Not by copying what others have done, but by carving our own paths, conscious of our unusual circumstances and the things we must do as a veritable act of creation, have we prepared ourselves to be, in miniature, a living pattern for the new peoples.

To insure that they derive the utmost benefit from that example, we must find room for more of their youth in our institutions of higher learning and special seminars, and facilitate practical training in our agricultural, co-operative, and educational undertakings. At the same time, we shall have to send them as many of our experts and instructors as we can spare, as we have begun to do in Burma, Ghana, Ethiopia, Nigeria, and elsewhere and recently also in Latin America. They must feel that they are performing a pioneer mission—not just a job for hire. This should be manifest in an attitude of humanity and fraternity, with neither arrogance nor self-deprecation, toward the peoples among whom they work, and an all-out effort to pass on the best of our knowledge and experience. Representatives of this type, and to our good fortune we have had them so far, will benefit both those they serve and Israel.

Israel, pre-eminently, needs and longs for closer fraternity and true co-operation between peoples. On her land borders, she is surrounded by hostility. She will be safe so long as her army is strong enough to deter her neighbors, but our heavy expenditure on defense slows down and circumscribes our progress in development and education. The surest way of arriving at peace and cooperation with our neighbors is not by proclaiming and preaching peace to the people of Israel, as certain naïve "peace-lovers" do, but by making the largest possible number of friends in Asia and Africa and elsewhere, who will understand Israel's capacity to assist the progress of developing peoples and convey that understanding to our neighbors. That purpose will not lessen our striving for co-operation and friendship with the peoples of Europe and America, where over 90 per cent of the Diaspora dwells: over five million in the United States, some three million in the Soviet Union, and two million in other parts. For many years those two continents, Europe and America, will still be the centers of the world's culture and science, and to satisfy the requirements of our security we must resort to them. Our relations with Asia and Africa will not loosen our ties with Europe and America but strengthen them. The moral precept in our Torah— "Thou shalt love thy neighbour as thyself"—accords with historic needs. The creative pioneering of Israel, which gave ampler substance to the dream of Jewish rebirth and salvation, will spur on new peoples by its example, guide them out of darkness, from penury to affluence, from dearth to plenty, and by enhancing Israel's prestige bring us nearer to peace with those about us.

We must be alive to the desperate attempts of Arab dictators to blacken Israel's name in Asia and Africa, and to upset fraternal relations established by co-operation between our emissaries and their peoples and by the experience of their representatives here. Our enemies are exploiting the most retrograde and fanatical elements of Islam, and Communist connivance as well. Our way will not be paved with easy, uninterrupted, and rapid successes. We have always had to fight hard and bitterly for things others got easily and without effort. Perhaps this is the secret of our moral and spiritual strength, our amazing vitality. We became a people noth-

ing can deter. Here and there we may fail. But so long as
we clearly comprehend the real meaning of the great
revolution being enacted before our eyes to bring about
not only the liberation of all peoples but a true partnership within the increasingly united family of mankind,
moving toward stable world peace, so long as we make
our contribution to it to the limit of the creativeness and
pioneering that are in us, no transient or localized troubles need check or unnerve us.

Three sublime ideals were put before us by Isaiah,
son of Amoz:

First—

> Fear not, for I am with thee;
> I will bring thy seed from the east,
> And gather thee from the west;
> I will say to the north: "Give up,"
> And to the south: "Keep not back,
> Bring My sons from far,
> And My daughters from the end of the earth.
>
> (Isaiah 43:5-6)

Second—

> I the Lord have called thee in righteousness,
> And have taken hold of thy hand,
> And kept thee, and set thee for a covenant of the
>   people,
> For a light of the nations.
>
> (Isaiah 42:6)

Third—

> And He shall judge between the nations,
> And shall decide for many peoples;

And they shall beat their swords into plowshares,
And their spears into pruning-hooks;
Nation shall not lift up sword against nation,
Neither shall they learn war any more.

(Isaiah 2:4)

Superficially, the three seem disparate, and in a fragmented world, with every region compartmentalized, it is doubtful whether any could have come true. The days of the Messiah are not yet, and the redemption of Jewry and mankind comes slowly. The miracles of science and technology in the first half of this century have cleared the way for a metamorphosis of humanity but entail many hazards. And yet, the footsteps of the Messiah are faintly to be heard even now: never before did our people see a return to Zion in such multitudes as in the early days of Israel's revival, though some millions still await it, many of them immured in exile.

The first signs are visible of the fulfillment of the prophecy "The root of Jesse, that standeth for an ensign of the people, unto him shall the nation seek." Youth from most of Africa and Asia, as well as the greatest European and America scientists, come to resurgent Israel to examine and emulate our methods for the advancement of new nations.

There is a great thirst in the world for true peace and a covenant of amity between the nations, and the more subject peoples are freed, to stand on their own feet and reinforce the United Nations, the stronger will be the pressure more speedily to quench that thirst. It is true that the independence of Asian and African peoples has become a new factor in interbloc tension, but these are "pangs of redemption." In our long journey through history we have known more suffering, more persecution, than any other people, but our faith in our future and in that of mankind has not been shaken, our hopes have not been blighted.

Even the Cold War is but a passing phase. Both the Soviet Union and the United States must obey the laws of change, and these two colossi will not forever face one another in militant challenge. In America the strength of the workers, be they laborers, farmers, or scientists, is rising; in the Soviet Union greater freedom and higher standards of living are sought, and as secondary and higher education expand there and the bonds between scientists everywhere draw tighter, the appetite for individual freedom, of thought, speech, and choice, will surely grow, and liberty will triumph in the end.

Today, when the United Nations is mentioned, the "United" is—not without cause—put in quotation marks. The member states are not yet united, and from time to time the Organization becomes a focus of international controversy. But unity of all nations is a paramount necessity, and unity—without quotation marks—will come *when all the peoples are free, internally and externally.* That it will come, even if it be slow in the coming, history decrees.

Israel must fight for this, for her security and future depend on the unity of nations, on the unity, freedom, and equality of all men.

She is a small country, with a small population, and wields no great military or economic power. In the long run, however, it is spiritual power that decides; in the kingdom of the spirit not quantity counts, but quality. It is not two or three Great Powers that will mold the world and determine its fate, but the historic needs of all the nations. Once the distinction between the ruling and dominant and the poor and backward nations is expunged, dictatorship will not last long, the danger of war will pass, confinement of peoples and populations against their will in totalitarian countries will cease, and the captives of Zion will return to their Homeland. And the Jewish people, which throughout its four thousand years of existence has believed in the supremacy of the spirit and in love for the stranger and sojourner, which has shown the tremendous things whereof creative human beings are capable when their steps are guided by a pioneering will and their path lit up by the Messianic vision of national and universal redemption—that people will behold the realization of the ideals of Isaiah, and its contribution to the establishment of the new world will bring it peace, security, and the world's respect, and will also strengthen world peace and human brotherhood.